DK EYEWITNESS TOP 10 TRAVEL GUIDES

ORLANDO

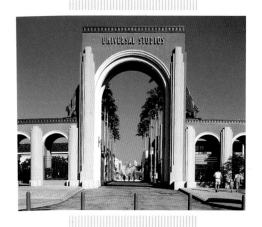

RICHARD GRULA
JIM & CYNTHIA TUNSTALL

DORLING KINDERSLEY
LONDON • NEW YORK • MUNICH
MELBOURNE • DELHI
WWW.DK.COM

Left **Mennello Museum** Center **Drag queen diva** Right **Merritt Island National Wildlife Preserve**

A DORLING KINDERSLEY BOOK

www.dk.com

Produced by Departure Lounge, London

Reproduced by Colourscan, Singapore
Printed and bound in Italy by Graphicom

First published in Great Britain in 2002
by Dorling Kindersley Limited
80 Strand, London WC2R 0RL
A Penguin Company

A CIP catalogue record is available from the British Library.

ISBN 0 7513 3904 0

Within each Top 10 list in this book, no hierarchy of quality or popularity is implied. All 10 are, in the editor's opinion, of roughly equal merit.

Contents

Orlando's Top 10

Key to abbreviations
Adm *admission charge payable* **DA** *disabled access*

Left **Water Mania** Center **Universal Studios** Right **Gatorland**

Left **SeaWorld Orlando** Right **Kennedy Space Center**

 Following pages **Incredible Hulk Ride, Islands of Adventure**

ORLANDO
TOP 10

ORLANDO'S TOP 10

TOP 10 Orlando's Highlights

One word describes Orlando's transformation in the last three decades: stunning. The city and its suburbs have gone through a Cinderella-like metamorphosis, where plain Jane has become a worldly beauty. Millions of tourists are seduced every year by sophisticated resorts, a wide range of theme parks, must-see attractions, happening nightclubs, and winning restaurants. Here are the Top 10 Orlando sights – Orlando's best of the best.

1 The Magic Kingdom Park

The park that started Disney's Florida empire combines fantasy, adventure, and the future in a package of rides and shows that focuses on Disney movies and TV programs. *See pp8–11.*

2 Epcot

Inquiring minds love this Disney park, which features technology in Future World and the culture, architecture and enticing food of 11 nations in World Showcase. *See pp12–15.*

3 Disney-MGM Studios

Lights, camera, action! Movies, TV shows and stomach-churning thrill rides come together in a theme park that sometimes also serves as a working studio. *See pp16–17.*

4 Disney's Animal Kingdom Park

Visitors are brought face to face with the wild world of animals, but this kingdom's spacious environmental design doesn't always offer a front-row seat. *See pp18–19.*

5 Islands of Adventure

Universal's top-of-the-pile theme park is a magnet for thrill jockeys, with some of the fastest, highest, and best rides in town. Be warned that 9 of its 13 rides have height or health restrictions, so it's not for the young, weak of stomach, or squeamish. *See pp20–23*

6 Universal Studios Florida
What Disney can do, Universal can equal. The movie and TV themes here can make people's wildest dreams come true or worst nightmares a (special effects) reality. From Jaws to Terminator, the silver screen comes to life. *See pp24–7.*

7 SeaWorld
Its laid-back pace, educational angle, and animal actors make this a popular stop for those wanting a break from the lines and stifling crowds at other parks. *See pp28–31.*

8 Wet 'n Wild
Some say it's hard to beat Disney's water parks, but this rival has the most thrills money can buy on the city's water scene. *See pp34–5.*

9 Cypress Gardens
Franklin Delaney Roosevelt was president when this park was created, but its southern belles and water-ski daredevils still make it a hit with millions of visitors every year. *See pp36–7.*

10 Kennedy Space Center
The appeal of man in space has turned America's No. 1 space center into a stellar attraction complete with live shuttle and rocket launches. *See pp38–41.*

Orlando's Top 10

For more on the Top 10 sights in Orlando See pp42–85

🔟 The Magic Kingdom® Park

Walt Disney's first Florida theme park opened in 1971, envisaged as a place where dreams could come true, even if only for a little while. It took six years and $400 million to create "Disneyland East," which has surpassed Walt's own dream: instead of being a spin-off of California's Disneyland Park, it has become the USA's most popular theme park, attracting more than 15 million visitors every year (some 40,000 each day). Although little has changed in 30 years, with more than 40 major attractions and countless minor ones, this is a true fantasy land for the young and young at heart.

🍗 A smoked turkey leg at Tomorrowland's Lunching Pad makes a good quick bite, but it's cheaper to bring your own snacks and water (bottles can be filled at the park's numerous fountains).

⏱ FastPass *(see p132),* cuts the amount of time spent standing in line for the park's most popular rides and shows.

The little publicized E Ride Nights let 5,000 people into the park at a reduced rate for three hours on select nights.

Consider visiting mid-week, as the park is at its busiest on weekends and early in the week.

As in all Disney parks, smoking is only allowed in designated outside areas.

🌐 World Drive • Map F1 • 407-824-4321 • www. disneyworld.com • Open at least 9am–7pm daily, call for seasonal hours. • Adm: adults $48, children (3–9) $38 (both plus 6% tax). Children under 3 go free.

Top 10 Attractions

1. Splash Mountain
2. Big Thunder Mountain Railroad
3. The Barnstormer at Goofy's Wiseacre Farm
4. Space Mountain
5. ExtraTERRORestrial Alien Encounter
6. Buzz Lightyear's Space Ranger Spin
7. The Many Adventures of Winnie the Pooh
8. Cinderella's Golden Carrousel
9. The Magic Carpets of Aladdin
10. Pirates of the Caribbean

1 Splash Mountain

Disney's 1946 film, *Song of the South*, inspires this wildly popular flume ride with Brer Rabbit leading the way through swamps, caves, and "the Laughing Place." Expect twists, turns, and a 52-ft (16-m), 45-degree, 40-mph (64-km) climax.

2 Big Thunder Mountain Railroad

Not the raciest of coasters, but the turns and dips, and realistic scenery, combine to make this an exciting trip on a runaway train through gold-rush country *(above).*

3 The Barnstormer at Goofy's Wiseacre Farm

Kids and some parents love this mini-roller coaster, which looks like a crop duster plane with Goofy at the controls.

4 Space Mountain

Orlando's first in-the-dark roller coaster is a ride on a rocket that shoots through hairpin turns and drops at what feels like breakneck speed, although top speed is only 28 mph (45 kmph). The cosmic effects and detail enhance this thrilling ride.

5 ExtraTERRORestrial Alien Encounter

If you like unexpected company, hang on tight as this George Lucas-created show sends an unearthly being into the space above and around you. It's dark, scary, confining – and then an alien spits on you.

6 Buzz Lightyear's Space Ranger Spin

Use the laser cannons on the dashboard to set off sight-and-sound effects as you hurtle through the sky and help *Toy Story's* most famous hero save the world.

7 The Many Adventures of Winnie the Pooh

Pooh, Eeyore, and a whole host of A. A. Milne's lovable characters come to life in this tranquil ride through the Hundred Acre Wood.

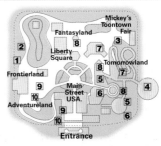

Magic Kingdom Park Plan

8 Cinderella's Golden Carrousel

This wonderfully refurbished 1917 carousel is a real beauty. It has handsome wooden horses and an organ that plays Disney classics. Kids love it, and adults love reminiscing about the rides of yesteryear.

Park Guide

Due to the crowds and distance involved, it takes around 20 minutes to get from the parking lots (via tram, boat, or monorail) to the park's attractions. Once inside, the Tip Board at the end of Main Street USA has the latest information on the length of lines and times of shows. Park maps are available from Guest Services to the left of the entrance. You'll need at least a day or parts of several to get the most out of the Magic Kingdom.

9 The Magic Carpets of Aladdin

This new Disney ride has four-passenger carpets which glide gently up and down and from side to side around a giant genie's bottle. But watch out for the sneaky, water-spitting camels.

10 Pirates of the Caribbean

Timbers are a-shiver as your boat cruises past a town under siege from a band of rum-soaked, Audio-Animatronic buccaneers. Dank dungeons, yo-ho-ho's, and brazen wenches – all scurvy pirate life is here.

Attraction number		1	2	3	4	5	6	7	8	9	10
Minimum height:	(inches)	40	40	35	44	44	–	–	–	–	–
	(cm)	102	102	89	112	112					
Recommended age group		8+	9+	4+	9+	9+	all	all	all	3+	3+
Duration (minutes)		10	4	1	3	18	5	4	2	3	8

For information on Disney's tour options See p129

Cinderella Castle with the Fantasy in the Sky Fireworks

TOP 10 Shows & Next Best Rides

1 Fantasy in the Sky Fireworks

This explosive show runs nightly during summer and holidays (occasionally at other times the year). Liberty Square, Mickey's Toontown Fair, and Frontierland are the best areas in the park to take in the fabulous display. If you want to view from outside the Magic Kingdom, Disney's Grand Floridian, Polynesian, Contemporary, and Wilderness Lodge resorts all have good views from upper floors.

2 Walt Disney World Railroad

The antique steam-driven trains that travel this 1.5-mile (2-km) perimeter track offer a good overview of the park's sights, but more importantly allow you to get from A to B without the legwork. It stops at City Hall, Main Street USA, Frontierland, and Mickey's Toontown Fair.

3 Cinderella Castle

Standing 185 ft (56 m) high, this park icon is a sight to behold. Complete with Gothic spires, it's the quintessential fairytale castle, reminiscent of Neuschwanstein, mad King Ludwig of Bavaria's creation. Inside, there's only one thing of interest to visitors, the Cinderella's Royal Table restaurant, where guests can partake of a character breakfast *(see p71)*.

4 Snow White's Scary Adventures

This ride lost some of its scary scenes with the evil queen and wicked witch to make it more enjoyable for smaller children. The queen still makes an appearance but is now joined by good-girl Snow White and the Prince.

5 It's a Small World

The insidious theme song will eat at your brain for months

after you visit, but small kids adore this slow-boat cruise through "lands" where small, Audio-Animatronic, costumed characters sing *It's a Small World After All* in their Munchkin-like voices.

6 Hall of Presidents

Every US president has an Audio-Animatronic likeness in this educational show that really high-lights the wizardry of Walt Disney Imagineers (designers). The pres-idents nod and wave, and Abe Lincoln is the keynote speaker.

7 Diamond Horseshoe Saloon Revue

This is a high-octane show at Dr. Bill U. Later's saloon. The curtain rises, and the town marshal sings and jokes with the audience, Miss Lucille L'Amour and her dance-hall girls can-can for dear life, while cowboys cavort energetically around the set.

8 Haunted Mansion

A corny yet fun special-effects show with a cult follow-ing. It's a slow-moving, slightly scary ride-in-the-dark that passes a ghostly ball, graveyard band, and weird flying objects.

9 Mickey & Minnie's Country Houses

In case you wondered, Mickey and his girlfriend don't cohabit. His place offers a wander-through visit of his garage and garden play-grounds, while next door, hers is a rather more hands-on experience.

Magic Kingdom Park Plan

10 Country Bear Jamboree

Audio-Animatronic bears croon and bellow songs in this knee-slapping revue. The finale has the audience hooting and clapping for an encore.

Magic Kingdom Parades

During summer (and occasionally at other times of the year) a key park event is the evening parade (times vary). The original show was the Main Street Electrical Parade, which was christened at California's Disneyland Park before moving to the Magic Kingdom in 1977. Its replacement is the bigger, better, and brighter SpectroMagic. This electri-fying, 20-minute extravaganza brings fountains, creatures, and floats filled with Disney characters to "light" It has no less than 204 speakers cranking out 72,000 watts, uses 75 tons of batter-ies (enough to power 90 houses for the duration), and 100 miles (160 km) of fiber-optic cable.The whole show is powered by 30 mini-computers. Arrive early and try to find a spot in front of the castle. If you can't stay until dark falls, there's a 15-minute Share the Dream Come Ture Parade (3pm daily) where guests can see their favorite Disney characters in a procession that leaves from Frontierland to finish off down Main Street USA.

Attraction number	1	2	3	4	5	6	7	8	9	10
Recommended age group	all	all	all	3+	3+	8+	all	8+	3–10	all
Duration (minutes)	20	20	–	3	11	30	45	8	–	17

TOP 10 Epcot®

Walt Disney imagined Epcot (Experimental Prototype Community of Tomorrow) as a futuristic township where people could live, work, and play in technologically enhanced splendor. After his death in 1966, the idea changed dramatically, and Epcot opened in 1982 as a park of two halves: Future World focuses on science, technology, and the environment, while World Showcase spotlights the cultures of several nations. The pairing works because both sections are educational and appeal to curious adults and kids alike. Be warned, the park is vast, a fact that has lead some to joke that its name is an acronym for "Every Person Comes Out Tired."

Future World: the Coral Reef in the Living Seas Pavilion is way better than most in-park restaurants *(see p95)*. Book ahead. World Showcase: Try fresh pastries at the Patisserie in the French Pavilion.

Use FastPass *(see p132)* a ride reservation system.

Save time and energy by using the shuttle boats to cross from Future World to the World Showcase.

This theme park is best toured in two days, if not more.

Epcot Center Dr, Walt Disney World Resort
• Map G2
• 407-824-4321
• www.disneyworld.com
• Future World: Opens 10am–7pm daily; World Showcase: Opens 11am–9pm daily. Hours are often extended during holidays and in summer months.
• Adm: adults $48, children (3–9) $38 plus tax. Children under 3 go free.

Top 10 Future World Exhibits

1. Test Track
2. Innoventions East
3. Innoventions West
4. The Living Seas
5. Universe of Energy
6. Honey, I Shrunk the Audience
7. Body Wars
8. Cranium Command
9. Spaceship Earth
10. Living with the Land

1 Test Track
Buckle up for a $60-dollar ride, created by a Disney-General Motors partnership. Riders in a six-passenger convertible car are taken through exhilarating brake tests, S-curves, and a 12-second, 65-mph (104-kmph) burst of speed. You must be at least 40 inches (102 cm) tall to ride.

2 Innoventions East
A refrigerator that can compile a grocery list and a toilet seat with a built-in warmer are among the "smart" furnishings in the House of Innoventions exhibit. Kids like this pavilion's Internet Zone with games such as virtual tag.

3 Innoventions West
Few can resist Video Games of Tomorrow, a Sega presentation that lets visitors try out next generation games. In the same pavilion, Medicine's New Vision is an exhibit that offers video games along a medical theme.

4 The Living Seas
Come face to face with sharks, barracudas, manatees, and more on a cinematic journey to an undersea laboratory. There are several hands-on exhibits including a deep sea diving suit that can be tried on.

5 Universe of Energy
A diverting show-and-ride that focuses on energy-related themes, from "fossil fuel" dinosaurs to future energy concerns.

6 Honey I Shrunk the Audience
Get ready to flinch during the Imagination Pavilion's larger-than-life film show. Seats vibrate as you're terrorized by giant mice. The family cat and dog, and a colossal 5-year-old also loom large before you "escape."

7 Body Wars
Hold tight as this Wonders of Life Pavilion show "reduces" you to the size of a cell for a shake, rattle, and roll rescue mission inside a human body (40-inch/102-cm minimum height).

Epcot Park Plan (Future World)

8 Cranium Command
Another entertaining Wonders of Life Pavilion show, this time exploring the workings of a typical 12-year-old boy's brain. The audience, sitting in a set that re-creates the inside of the kid's head, is right there with him as he endures the trials of an average pre-teen day.

9 Spaceship Earth
The ride inside is nothing to write home about. But, this giant golf ball – actually a 180-ft (55-m) geosphere *(above)* – is an engineering marvel, made of 11,324 triangular aluminum panels that absorb the rain rather than letting it run off.

10 Living with the Land
The best of the vast Land Pavilion's exhibits involves a boat ride through rain forest, desert, and prairie biomes. It's followed by a look at agricultural experiments including hydroponics and growing plants in simulated Martian soil.

Park Guide

The main entrance is convenient for Future World, where nine pavilions encircle Spaceship Earth. Getting to World Showcase Lagoon and the 11 nations beyond requires a longer trek, though handy boat shuttles run from Showcase Plaza to the pavilions of Germany and Morocco. A second entrance, at International Gateway, is accessible from Disney's Yacht Club, Beach Club, and BoardWalk Inn resorts. Maps that give up-to-date show information are available at both entrances.

Attraction number	1	2	3	4	5	6	7	8	9	10
Recommended age group	8+	8+	8+	all	all	all	8+	8+	all	all
Duration (minutes)	5	–	–	30	32	9	5	20	17	13

For science on a smaller scale at the Orlando Science Center **See p111**

Norway Pavilion

TOP10 World Showcase Pavilions

1 Canada
The star attraction here is the inspirational 360-degree CircleVision film, *O Canada!*, which reveals some of the country's scenic wonders. You also get to experience traveling by dogsled. Outside, Canada's rugged terrain is convincingly re-created. Gardens that are based on Victoria's Butchart gardens, a replica of an Indian village, and the Northwest Mercantile store, selling items such as tribal crafts and Canadian maple syrup, can be explored.

2 China
The CircleVision movie, *Wonders of China*, is a fascinating journey through China's natural and man-made riches. The pavilion features a 15th-century Ming dynasty temple, a ceremonial gate, and tranquil gardens. The Yong Feng Shangdian Department Store *(see p92)* is a wonderful treasure trove of Asian goodies. Try not to miss the dynamic Dragon Legend Acrobats who perform several times each day.

3 Morocco
Look for the Koutoubia minaret, a copy of the tower from a 12th-century mosque in Marrakesh, and you've found this exotic pavilion. Inside, the typical souk architecture is embellished by beautiful carvings and mosaics. The Casbah marketplace *(see p92)* is bursting with hard-to-resist crafts sold by "merchants," and you can see carpets being woven on looms. "Local" cuisine such as couscous is available in the Pavilion's restaurant *(see p97)*.

4 American Adventure
Enhance your knowledge of US history in a 30-minute dramatization featuring Audio-Animatronic actors. Mark Twain and Benjamin Franklin are the narrators who explain key events, including the

writing of the Declaration of Independence, and Susan B. Anthony speaks out for women's rights. The Voices of Liberty singers perform in the main hall of the pavilion, which is modeled on Philadelphia's Liberty Hall.

5 Japan

A breathtaking five-story pagoda, based on Nara's 8th-century Horyuji temple, forms the centerpiece of this architecturally amazing pavilion. The traditional Japanese gardens are pretty impressive, too, and a perfect spot to escape the throngs. The peace and quiet is only occasionally broken by the beat of drums: go investigate: the Matsuriza troupe is one of the best shows in Epcot.

6 Norway

Norway's Maelstrom ride takes you on a 10-minute journey through fiords and fairy-tale forests in a dragon-headed vessel. You land in a 10th-century Viking village, where a short film portrays Norway's natural treasures. The realistic replica of Oslo's 14th-century Akershus Castle houses the restaurant *(see p97)*.

7 United Kingdom

Examples of typical British architecture through the ages line the quaint cobblestone streets here. Apart from shops selling quintessential British merchandise

Illuminations

Created to celebrate the new millennium, Epcot's stunning fireworks and laser show is still thrilling visitors every night at 9pm. It is a grand half-hour, sound-and-vision nightcap which also brings the World Showcase Lagoon fountains into the act. There are scores of good viewing places all around the edge of the Lagoon.

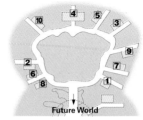

Future World

Epcot Park Plan (World Showcase)

(teas, china, crystal, and more), there's also a park with a bandstand and Beatles impersonators providing entertainment.

8 Mexico

El Rio del Tiempo (River of Time) is an eight-minute multimedia boat ride that explores Mexico's past and present, from the Yucatan's Mayan pyramids (the pavilion is housed in a replica of one) to the urban bustle of Mexico City life. Mariachis entertain, and there's a *plaza* with stalls selling colorful souvenirs such as sombreros, *piñatas*, and leather goods.

9 France

This pavilion sports scale replicas, including the Eiffel Tower, and shops selling French products. The 18-minute, five-screen film, which sweeps through glorious landscapes accompanied by the music of French composers is a highlight.

10 Germany

In this cartoon-like, archetypal German village, you'll find a miniature model railroad, including a wonderfully detailed Bavarian Village. The Biergarten restaurant (complete with brass band) serves traditional food, and shops sell everything from Hummel figurines to wines and cuckoo clocks.

📖 Disney-MGM Studios

Like Universal Studios, Disney-MGM Studios underscores Orlando's standing as a small, but growing, film production center and offers an up-close look at the world of "Lights! Camera! Action!". The park cost $300 million to create and the result is an effective fusion of fun and information; the attractions tend to be complex, involving rides, shows, and educational commentary, so there really is something for everyone. Nostalgic references to Hollywood's heyday are balanced by high-tech trickery, making this a must for anyone with even a remote interest in the movies.

🍦 A hand-dipped ice-cream cone at Hollywood Scoops slides down a treat, but for more substantial refreshment, try the Sci-Fi Dine-In Theater, serving diner fare in a 1950s retro setting, where guests can watch B-movie clips.

⏱ Use FastPass *(see p132)*, a ride reservation system, to cut the amount of time spent standing in line for the most popular rides and shows.

As in all Disney parks, smoking is only allowed in designated outdoor areas.

The Magic of Disney Animation is a tour that takes you behind the Fantasmic! scenes and lets you try your hand at painting an animation cel. Call 407-939-8687.

🦅 *Epcot Resorts Blvd*
• *Map G2*
• *407-824-4321*
• *www.disneyworld.com*
• *Open at least 9am–7pm, sometimes later*
• *Adm: adults $48, children (3–9) $38 (both plus 6% tax), children under three go free.*

Top 10 Attractions

1. Rock 'n' Roller Coaster Starring Aerosmith
2. Twilight Zone™ Tower of Terror
3. Fantasmic!
4. Indiana Jones™ Epic Stunt Spectacular
5. Jim Henson's Muppet* Vision 3-D
6. Disney-MGM Studios Backlot Tour
7. Who Wants to Be a Millionaire – Play It!
8. Star Tours
9. Beauty and the Beast Live on Stage
10. Hunchback of Notre Dame: A Musical Adventure

1 Rock 'n' Roller Coaster Starring Aerosmith

A sign warns, "prepare to merge as you've never merged before," but by then it's too late. Your limo zooms from 0 to 60 mph (97 kmph) in 2.8 seconds and into multiple inversions as Aerosmith blares at 32,000 watts *(above)*.

2 Twilight Zone™ Tower of Terror

The spooky surroundings are a façade in front of the real terror, a gut-tightening, 13-story fall. To many, it's Disney's best thrill ride.

3 Fantasmic!

Lasers, fireworks, waterborne images, and a sorcerer mouse are the stars of this end-of-day extravaganza that pits the forces of good against Disney villains such as Cruella De Ville and Maleficent. Performance times vary seasonally.

4 Indiana Jones™ Epic Stunt Spectacular

Indy's action-packed day is full of thrills and spills, and near-death encounters. A stunt co-ordinator explains how it's all done.

5 Jim Henson's Muppet*Vision 3-D

Miss Piggy, Kermit, and the rest of the crew star in a show celebrating both Henson's legacy and Disney's special-effects wizardry and audio-animatronics.

6 Disney-MGM Studios Backlot Tour

What begins as a tram tour through movie sets and the prop department ends at Catastrophe Canyon. Here, explosions, floods, and fire give riders a bit of a shake-up before getting to see behind the Canyon's scenes.

7 Who Wants to Be a Millionaire – Play It!

Sorry, no cash is involved. But the theme park version of this TV game show gives contestants a shot at 15 multiple-choice questions and a chance to win prizes, including a trip to New York to see a taping of the real show.

Disney-MGM Studios Park Plan

8 Star Tours

Climb in and swallow hard: your 40-seat spacecraft is going on a journey riddled with dips, bumps, and laser fire. The ride's technology may be a bit outdated, but forgiving Star Wars fans still say this ride hits the spot.

Park Guide

Pick up a map from Guest Services, to the left of the entrance. Staff are on hand to help you find your way around and provide information. The tip board at Sunset and Hollywood boulevards lists up-to-the-minute information on show schedules, wait times, visiting celebrities, and ride or show closures. This park tends to be less busy at the beginning of the week, when many visitors hit the Magic Kingdom or Epcot, and it can easily be tackled in one day.

9 Beauty and the Beast Live on Stage!

The music from the animated film alone is enough to sell this Broadway-style show. The sets, costumes, and production numbers are pretty spectacular, too.

10 Hunchback of Notre Dame: A Musical Adventure

Puppets, real actors, and lots of catchy music and songs bring the famous story of hunchback Quasimodo's love for Esmeralda alive in this open-air show.

Attraction number		1	2	3	4	5	6	7	8	9	10
Minimum height	(inches)	48	40	–	–	–	–	–	40	–	–
	(cm)	122	101						101		
Recommended age group		9+	9+	all	all	all	all	8+	8+	all	all
Duration (minutes)		3.5	4.5	30	40	25	35	30	10	30	32

TOP 10 Disney's Animal Kingdom® Park

As the name implies, wildlife rules at the latest addition to Disney's empire of fun. Here, the serious issue of conservation is combined with the playfulness of a theme park, though critics complain that the landscaping makes it hard to see the animals, especially in the hottest parts of the day. There's compensation in the fact that the park has some enthraling shows and rides, and rumor has it that future plans for a new zone include a roller coaster. For now, the park is all about getting back to nature, albeit of a more exotic kind than the one Florida usually has to offer.

🍴 Roasted corn from the Chakranadi Chicken Shop makes a great snack.

⏰ The best times to see the animals are as soon as the park opens and within an hour of it closing, especially during the hot months (May–Sep).

Use FastPass *(see p132)*, a ride reservation system that helps cut the amount of time spent standing in line for the most popular rides and shows.

As in all Disney parks, smoking is allowed only in designated outdoor areas.

🌐 *Savannah Circle, Walt Disney World Resort*
• *Map G1*
• *407-824-4321*
• *www.disneyworld.com*
• *open at least 8am–6pm, sometimes 7am–7pm. Call for seasonal hours.*
• *Adm: adults $48, children (3–9) $38 plus tax. Children (under 3) go free.*

Top 10 Attractions

1. Kilimanjaro Safaris
2. Pangani Forest Exploration Trail
3. Festival of The Lion King
4. Kali River Rapids
5. Maharajah Jungle Trek
6. Tree of Life
7. It's Tough to Be a Bug!
8. Tarzan™ Rocks!
9. Dinosaur
10. The Boneyard

1 Kilimanjaro Safaris

The park's most popular ride *(right)* puts you on a large safari jeep to bump along dirt tracks looking for black rhinos, lions, zebras, and more. You're reminded that it's a theme park, though, as a staged adventure unfolds – guests have to save the elephants from "poachers." The animals are real, but that baobab tree was made by talented Disney artists, known as Imagineers.

2 Pangani Forest Exploration Trail

As you're surrounded by thick vegetation, it's sometimes hard to see the animals on this walk-in-the-woods with a difference. The gorillas are the main attraction, but if the stars of the show prove shy, there are also hippos, exotic birds, and weird-looking mole-rats.

3 Festival of The Lion King

One of Orlando's best shows won't fail to throw you into the spirit of things when it gets going. This production uses singers, dancers, and The Lion King's popular score to emphasize nature's diversity.

4 Kali River Rapids

The park's conservation message is evident on this exciting raft ride, which passes from a lush landscape to one in the process of being scorched for logging. You need to be 38 inches (96 cm) tall or more to ride, and like to get wet!

For other Disney sights and attractions See pp88–91

5 Maharajah Jungle Trek
The giant Old World fruit bats, some with man-sized wingspans, are easily spotted, but the Bengal tigers are elusive when it's hot. You might also see Komodo dragons, tapirs, and deer on this atmospheric Asian stroll.

6 Tree of Life
The park's symbol is this 145-ft (44-m) tall tree created by Walt Disney Imagineers. Look carefully: there are 325 mammals, reptiles, amphibians, insects, birds, dinosaurs, and Mickeys carved into its trunk, limbs, and roots.

Disney's Animal Kingdom Park Plan

7 It's Tough to Be a Bug!
Located inside the Tree of Life's 50-ft (15-m) base, this 3-D, effect-filled show offers a view of the world from an insect's perspective. The climax is sure to make an impression.

8 Tarzan™ Rocks!
Dancers, tumblers, and daring (often aerial) in-line skaters wearing spectacular costumes are all part of this exhila-rating show, although it's Phil Collins' music that really gets the audience rocking.

9 Dinosaur
Expect to be shaken up on this wild ride, which takes you back 65 million years. Convincing animatronic dinosaurs lurk in the darkness. There's a 40-inch (102-cm) minimum height requirement.

10 The Boneyard
Possibly the best of its kind in any of the Disney Parks, this playground is a perfect place for kids to burn off surplus energy. The play area is built around the "remains" of dinosaurs. It's both educational and fun.

Park Guide
The park, which is Walt Disney World Resort's largest, is divided into six zones: Oasis (the entrance area); Discovery Island (with the Tree of Life at its center); and the lands of Camp Minnie-Mickey (the main children's zone), Africa, Asia, and Dinoland USA radiating out from it. Maps are available at Guest Relations, at the entrance to the park.

Attraction number	1	2	3	4	5	6	7	8	9	10
Recommended age group	all	all	all	8+	all	all	all	all	9+	3 to 12
Duration (minutes)	14	–	28	5	–	–	7	28	4	–

For another conservation-oriented park See pp28–31

🔟 Islands of Adventure

Orlando didn't have a lot to offer adrenalin junkies until Universal unveiled its second Central Florida park in 1999. Billed as the "world's most technologically advanced theme park," no local rivals can touch Islands of Adventure's (IOA) thrill power and innovation (although Tampa's Busch Gardens [see p82] is also highly rated by thrill-seekers). With terrifying roller coasters, three heart-stopping water attractions, and stunningly creative rides, it is the place to head for those who like to live dangerously.

Green Eggs and Ham Café

🟢 Go on. Try a green eggs and ham sandwich at the Green Eggs and Ham Café.

🟠 The Universal Express system *(see p132)* cuts the amount of time spent standing in line for the most popular rides and shows.

Some of the park's rides have shorter lines for single guests and couples willing to split up.

During thunderstorms, the park's plentiful outdoor rides close.

🔎 *Hollywood Way*
• Map T1 • 407-363-8000 • www.universal orlando.com
• Open at least 9am–7pm, call for seasonal hours.
• Adm: adults $48, children (3–9) $39 (both plus 6% tax), children under three go free.
• One-day tickets can be upgraded to a two-day pass if you find you want to spend another day in the park.

Top 10 Attractions

1 Incredible Hulk Coaster
2 The Amazing Adventures of Spider-Man
3 Doctor Doom's Fearfall
4 Pteranodon Flyers
5 Jurassic Park River Adventure
6 Popeye & Bluto's Bilge-Rat Barges
7 Dudley Do-Right's Ripsaw Falls
8 Dueling Dragons
9 Poseidon's Fury: Escape from the Lost City
10 The Cat in the Hat

2 The Amazing Adventures of Spider-Man
Slap on 3-D glasses and battle the baddies while fireballs and other computer-generated objects fly at you. The technology is amazing *(below)*.

3 Doctor Doom's Fearfall
This ride climbs 200 ft (61 m), before dropping and pausing at several levels to maximum thrilling effect.

4 Pteranodon Flyers
Eye-catching metal gondolas swing from side to side on this prehistoric bird's-eye tour around the park's Jurassic Park zone.

1 Incredible Hulk Coaster
You blast out of the darkness at 40 mph (64 kmph), go weightless, and endure seven inversions and two drops during this white-knuckle ride *(below)*.

5 Jurassic Park River Adventure
This ride starts slowly but quickly picks up speed as some raptors get loose *(below)*. To escape you will have to take an 85-ft (26-m), flume-style plunge.

6 Popeye & Bluto's Bilge-Rat Barges
The water is freezing on what is Florida's bounciest raft ride. Expect to be squirted, splashed, or even drenched as your 12-passenger "barge" goes the course.

7 Dudley Do-Right's Ripsaw Falls
Six-passenger logs cruise the lagoon before giving riders an excuse for a good squeal, a steep drop at 50 mph (80 kmph). The ride seems to finish up "underwater."

Islands of Adventure Park Plan

Park Guide
Despite the elevators and moving sidewalks, it can still take 20 minutes to get to the attractions from the parking lot. Try to arrive early; if you are staying in a Universal Resort, you can get in before other visitors. Despite the predominance of scary rides, the park's Seuss Landing will keep younger kids happy. Maps for a handy boat shuttle, which links Port of Entry and Jurassic Park, are available at Guest Relations to the right of the Port of Entry.

8 Dueling Dragons
These two floorless coasters do five rollovers and come within 1 ft (30 cm) of each other no less than three times. If you are really courageous, go for seats in the front row.

9 Poseidon's Fury: Escape from the Lost City
Pass through a swirling vortex of water, then look on as all hell breaks loose when Poseidon and Zeus have an almighty battle.

10 The Cat in the Hat
Hold on as your couch spins and turns through 18 Seussian scenes. The Cat, Thing One, and Thing Two join you on a ride through a day that's anything but ordinary.

Attraction number		1	2	3	4	5	6	7	8	9	10
Minimum height:	(inches)	54	40	52	36	42	42	44	54	–	–
	(cm)	137	102	132	91	107	107	112	137	–	–
Recommended age group		9+	8+	10+	7+	9+	9+	9+	9+	all	8+
Duration (minutes)		2	4	0.5	1.5	6.5	6.5	5.5	2.5	6	5

21

Left **One Fish, Two Fish....** Center **Dudley Do-Right** Right **Jurassic Park Discovery Center**

🔟 Gentler Attractions

1 One Fish, Two Fish, Red Fish, Blue Fish

Fly your fish up, down, and all around on an aerial carousel ride just 15 ft (4 m) off the ground. If you don't do what the song says, you'll get sprayed with water.

2 Caro-Seuss-El

This merry-go-round replaces the traditional horses with interactive versions of Dr. Seuss's cowfish, elephant birds, and mulligatawnies. Regular carousels will never seem the same again.

3 If I Ran the Zoo

The 19 interactive stations in this Seussian playground use features such as flying water snakes, caves, and water cannons, and include a place to tickle the toes of a Seussian critter.

4 Jurassic Park Discovery Center

See through a dinosaur's eyes, match your DNA to theirs, and watch an animatronic velociraptor "hatch" in the laboratory. There are several interactive stations, where kids can brush up on their dinosaur facts.

5 Triceratops Encounter

"She" is a 24-ft- (7-m) long, 10-ft- (3-m) high animatronic *Triceratops* dinosaur that blinks, breathes, emits a hooting cry,

Triceratops Encounter

and lets some guests touch her. Visit her in her paddock and listen to "trainers" talk about her care.

6 Camp Jurassic

Burn off energy in an adventure playground full of places to explore, including dark caves where "spitters" (small dinosaurs) lurk. See if you can find out how to make dinosaurs roar.

7 Me Ship, The Olive

The play area here is full of interactive fun, while Cargo Crane offers an alternative hands-on experience: a chance to fire water cannons at riders on Popeye & Bluto's Bilge-Rat Barges (see p21).

8 Flying Unicorn

Dueling Dragons (see p21) it ain't. This kiddie coaster has a gentle corkscrew action. Riders must be 36 inches (90 cm) tall.

9 Mystic Fountain

This child-pleaser is a seeing, talking fountain, which surprises then captivates most of those who see it.

10 Storm Force Accelatron

Dizziness is the name of the game as you and X-Men superhero Storm spin your vehicle fast enough to create electrical energy that will send the evil Magneto to the great beyond.

Top 10 Facts

1. Steven Spielberg produced the 3-D films shown in Spider-Man.
2. Spider-Man's screens are up to 90 ft (27 m) wide.
3. The 15-Hz square audio wave shock used in Spider-Man is a frequency low enough to make humans sick.
4. Each "Scoop" on the Spider-Man ride actually only moves 12 inches (30 cm) up or down.
5. Dueling Dragons' Fire Dragon can travel at up to 60 mph (96 kmph), the Ice Dragon at up to 55 mph (88 kmph).
7. Dueling Dragons' structure is 3,200 ft (975 m) long and can handle 3,264 riders per hour.
8. At 3,180 ft (969 m), Dueling Dragons' line is the longest in the world.
9. The Hulk is 3,700 ft (1.1 km) long and can handle 1,920 riders per hour.
10. The Hulk's G-force is the same as that experienced in a F-16 fighter jet attack.

IOA's "State-of-the-Future" Rides

Guests at Islands of Adventure (IOA) get a first-hand demonstration of some of the most technologically advanced coasters and attractions ever created. At the top of the list is The Amazing Adventures of Spider-Man (see p20), a ride that took half a decade and more than $100 million to develop. New digital film technologies had to be invented for the convincing floor-to-ceiling 3-D images that are projected to a moving audience. The "Scoop" motion simulator, wind cannons, and pyrotechnics are precision-synchronized by a vast computer network. Computers also play a big part in the Dueling Dragons ride (see p21). They calculate the weight of every passenger load, then adjust the speed and departure sequence in order to maximize thrills on this duel coaster. Unique to the Incredible Hulk Coaster (see p20) is a thrust system that blasts cars out of a tunnel instead of the usual long, slow haul to the top of an incline. But even with all these high-tech innovations, some low-tech touches can't be avoided. Just below the Hulk stretches a huge net designed to catch personal belongings that fall from screaming riders.

The Incredible Hulk

Riders experience zero-gravity inversions as they are spun upside down at 110 ft (33 m) above the ground before dropping 105 ft (32 m) at more than 60 mph (96 kmph)

The Amazing Adventures of Spider-Man

23

Universal Studios Florida

Universal's first park in Florida opened in 1990, with movie-themed rides and shows, and a mission to steal some of Disney-MGM's limelight. But it is only since a recent revamp that the park has really taken off, due largely to the runaway success of the latest additions, the hugely popular Men in Black Alien Attack, Terminator 2: 3-D, and the child-friendly Woody Woodpecker's KidZone.

The Universal globe

🍩 Don your movie star shades and grab a pastry and a cappuccino at the Beverly Hills Boulangerie.

🎬 The Universal Express ticket *(see p132)* lets you cut the amount of time spent in lines for the most popular rides and shows.

VIP tours *(see p129)* help beat the crowds during peak periods.

Note that some rides don't open until around 11am.

🌐 1000 Universal Studios Plaza
• Map T1
• 407-363-8000
• www.universalorlando. com
• Open at least 9am–7pm but call to check seasonal hours.
• Adm: adults $48, children (3–9) $39 (both plus 6% tax), children under 3 go free.

Top 10 Attractions

1. Terminator 2: 3-D
2. Back to the Future – The Ride
3. Men in Black Alien Attack
4. Twister – Ride It Out
5. Kongfrontation
6. Jaws
7. Earthquake – The Big One
8. Hitchcock's 3-D Theater
9. FUNtastic World of Hanna-Barbera
10. Nickelodeon Studios Tour

1 Terminator 2: 3-D
Live stage action, six 8-ft (2.4-m) robots, and an amazing three-screen, 3-D film *(below)* combine for a stunning, action-packed show (PG-13).

2 Back to the Future – The Ride
This head-spinning motion simulator puts original cast member Christopher Lloyd on screen, urging you through some scary mind-altering moments in space.

3 Men in Black Alien Attack
You and your "alienator" must keep the intergalactic bad guys from taking over the world as you spin through the streets, looking to shoot the monstrous bugs *(below)*.

4 Twister – Ride It Out
The special effects make you feel as if a tornado is sucking the air out of the room as a 5-story funnel cloud really does make cows fly. Rated PG-13.

5 Kongfrontation
A tram cruises the streets while a 40-ft- (12.2-m) tall monster Kong pounds on the roof – among other things. A bit corny but still fun.

For Universal's sister park, Islands of Adventure, **See pp20–23**

6 Jaws

A leisurely boat tour turns into a nightmare when a large dorsal fin appears and Jaws attacks. This $45-million ride is even scarier after dark, but the special effects are spectacular at any time of the day.

Universal Studios Florida Park Plan

7 Earthquake – The Big One

All hell breaks loose when a San Francisco subway car is hit by a massive quake. Amazing effects include explosions and a catastrophic flood.

Park Guide

It takes about 20 minutes to get from the parking lot to the attractions. Once inside, if you feel disoriented, park hosts can advise you on how best to get from A to B. If you are staying at a Universal hotel, make use of the early admission perk; if you haven't got that option, try to arrive an hour before the park opens and hit the major rides first. The park tends to be quietest midweek, and the crowds seem to evaporate when it rains, so this park is a good bet in bad weather. While it's mostly a built up mix of soundstages, backlots, sets, and shops, there are some green areas in which to take time out.

8 Hitchcock's 3-D Theater

In this PG-13-rated tribute to the late master, *The Birds* come to life in 3-D and the audience visits *Psycho*'s famous shower scene. Expect some audience participation.

9 FUNtastic World of Hanna-Barbera

Captain Yogi leads riders on a wild (he's not the best pilot) simulator ride to save cartoon character Elroy Jetson from a kidnapping orchestrated by Dick Dastardly. Great fun.

10 Nickelodeon Studios Tour

This behind-the-scenes tour also offers the ultimate parental revenge: get your kid "slimed" by telling them to volunteer when the Master of Ceremonies asks for helpers.

Attraction number		1	2	3	4	5	6	7	8	9	10
Minimum height:	(inches)	–	42	40	–	–	–	–	–	40	–
	(cm)		107	102						102	
Recommended age group		all	8+	8+	8+	8+	8+	8+	8+	5+	all
Duration (minutes)		23	4	4	18	5	20	5	30	4	45

For more attractions in the International Drive area See pp96–9

Left **A Day in the Park with Barney** Right **Beetlejuice's Rock 'n Roll Graveyard Revue**

🔟 Shows & Kids' Stuff

1 Wild, Wild, Wild West Stunt Show

Stunt teams show off their thrills and spills during an 18-minute show that reveals how stuntmen survive dynamite explosions and three-story falls. Take notice of the splash warning!

2 Beetlejuice's Rock 'n Roll Graveyard Revue

Dracula, Wolfman, Frankenstein, and Beetlejuice rock the house with music and pyrotechnic special effects in an 18-minute show. Rated PG-13.

3 The Gory, Gruesome & Grotesque Horror Make-Up Show

Ever wanted to know how they did the transformation scenes in *The Fly* and *The Exorcist*? Here's your chance to learn. The 20-minute show is rated PG-13.

4 Blues Brothers

Non-purist fans of this film, who don't need to see John Belushi and Dan Ackroyd in the key roles, will enjoy this foot-stomping 20-minute revue.

5 Animal Planet Live!

The park's newest show features wild, wacky, and occasionally weird live and video animal action. Expect plenty of audience participation.

6 Woody Woodpecker's Nuthouse Coaster

Very similar to the Barnstormer ride in Disney's Magic Kingdom *(see p8)*, this 55-second ride for the young (and timid adults) has just one corkscrew curve.

7 E. T. Adventure

Everyone's favorite extra-terrestrial takes guests on a bike ride to save his planet. Peddle through strange landscapes to meet Tickli Moot Moot and other characters that Steven Spielberg created for this ride.

8 A Day in the Park with Barney

The puffy purple dinosaur is adored by preschool kids, so this 25-minute sing-along show is guaranteed to get small fans into a frenzy. Everyone else should probably steer clear.

9 Fievel's Playland

This partially hidden water playground has a house for kids to explore and a mini water slide, for which the line is often painfully slow.

10 The Boneyard

It won't make the highlight reel, but this area is worth a look for film buffs. It contains an oft-changing display of props and set pieces from some of Universal's more memorable movies.

Fievel's Playland

For Orlando's best dinner shows See pp80–81

Top 10 TV shows and Films made at Universal Studios Florida

1 Nickelodeon
2 Parenthood (1989)
3 Oscar (1990)
4 Psycho IV (1990)
5 Problem Child 2 (1991)
6 Matinee (1992)
7 The Waterboy (1998)
8 Hoover (1998)
9 House on Haunted Hill (1999)
10 Held for Ransom (2000)

Behind the scenes

Universal Studios Florida is more than just a tourist attraction. It is also the state's largest full-service studio facility and the heart of central Florida's burgeoning film and television production industry – an industry that rings Orlando's cash registers to the tune of nearly $500 million dollars annually. It's easy to see why the city is firmly in contention for the nickname "Hollywood East." Since opening in 1988, Universal Studios Florida has been the production site for more than 2,000 television shows, commercials, music videos, and movies. As well as nine enormous soundstages, there are plenty of locations around the park that are used for filming, from downtown Manhattan to the Wild West. If park guests want to be part of some camera action, they can join the studio audience when TV shows shoot episodes at Universal. Tickets for these productions are typically distributed free of charge on the day of taping. Visitors can check in advance with Guest Services to find out if special event TV shows will be taped during their visit; shooting boards and the park map should also give up-to-date details.

Star Spotting

Universal Studios doesn't just allow you to "ride the movies." Here, you get to meet the stars, too. Actors playing a whole host of silver screen legends and characters including the Marx Brothers, Marilyn Monroe, Charlie Chaplin, and the Flintstones can be seen around the park (especially in the Front Lot) and are always willing to pose for photos.

Hollywood Boulevard, Universal Studios Florida

TOP 10 SeaWorld Orlando

Opened in 1973, SeaWorld Orlando is the city's third major attraction. But its unique marine wildlife focus and educational goals puts it in a league all of its own. Guests can get up close and personal with killer whales, sea lions, manatees, rays, and a host of other watery creatures. The recent thrill ride additions have expanded the park's appeal to teens, confirming SeaWorld as an essential part of any family's Orlando visit.

Journey to Atlantis ride

🍽 For lunch, try the Deli at the Anheuser-Busch Hospitality Center. The sandwiches are large and the first two draft beers are free (that's the limit per person).

🎫 Get a SeaWorld Express ticket for special access *(see p132)*.

Beat the heat with mid-day visits to air-conditioned indoor attractions.

Didn't bring a stroller? Rent one at the Children's Store. Two-way radios can also be hired at the maps & education building.

⊗ 7007 SeaWorld Dr
• Map T5
• 1-800-327-2424
• www.seaworld.com
• Opens 9am, closes between 5pm and 10pm (depending on the season)
• Adm: adults $47.95, children (3–9) $38.95 (plus 6% tax). Children under 3 go free.

Top 10 Attractions

1. Shamu Adventure
2. Wild Arctic
3. Kraken
4. Journey to Atlantis
5. Clyde & Seamore Take Pirate Island
6. Terrors of the Deep
7. Manatees: The Last Generation?
8. Pacific Point Preserve
9. Dolphin Cove
10. Intensity Water Ski Show

Wild Arctic
2 An impressive and chilly re-creation of the Arctic, with polar bears *(below)*, beluga whales, and walruses. Guests can opt to "arrive" by a simulated helicopter ride, but the line will be longer.

Kraken
3 Billed as the "tallest, fastest, longest, and only floorless roller coaster in Orlando," Kraken is a fearsome thrill. It takes riders up 15 stories, spins them upside down seven times, and goes under water, all at speeds up to 65 mph (104.6 kmph).

Shamu Adventure
1 The park's best live show. Killer whales *(below)* fling trainers in the air, beach themselves close to the crowd, and splash the first 14 rows of the audience.

Journey to Atlantis
4 The big draw of this flume ride is a 60-ft (18-m) drop, but the surprise bonus is the twisting roller coaster section near the end. Everyone should expect to get wet, especially those in the front of the car.

Clyde & Seamore Take Pirate Island
5 This swashbuckling live-action comedy features a cast of mischievous sea lions and otters who steal the show from their human co-stars.

For more watery fun in Orlando See pp48–9

SeaWorld Orlando Park Plan

6 Terrors of the Deep

Here, thanks to the world's largest underwater acrylic tunnel, you can stand six inches (15 cm) from a toothy shark and glide on a people-mover through a world of slithery eels, pufferfish, and sleek barracuda.

7 Manatees: The Last Generation?

The hulking "sea cow" is one of the Earth's gentlest creatures but endangered due to injuries from boat propellers. This exhibit has above- and below-water viewing of those brought here to recuperate.

8 Pacific Point Preserve

On the surf-drenched rocks of this re-created California coast, hundreds of sea lions and seals cavort and squall in a deafening, endless request for lunch.

Park Guide

Upon arrival, grab a map/event schedule at the Information Counter, and plan your visit according to the live shows you wish to see. The thrill rides – Wild Arctic, Kraken, and Journey To Atlantis – have the longest lines, so visit those when major live shows are taking place. Finally, consider visiting in the late afternoon and evening. Lines vanish, temperatures cool, and the park takes on a different character under the evening sky.

9 Dolphin Cove

The spirit of "Flipper" lives on with these playful bottlenose dolphins *(left)*, which romp at the edge of a lagoon where they can be petted. The underwater viewing area is the best spot to see them in action.

10 Intensity Water Ski Show

No wildlife here – just world-class water-skiers and wake-boarders who compete in an extreme sports bonanza. Between events, SeaWorld water-skiers dazzle with acrobatics and aquabatics.

Left **Dolphin Nursery** Right **Penguin Encounter**

TOP 10 Shows & Other Attractions

1 Pets Ahoy
A multi-species cast of 18 cats, a dozen dogs, a flock of birds, a den of rats, three little pigs, and one horse prove their stage savvy in this humorous display of skills and tricks.

2 Shamu Close Up
The underwater viewing area for SeaWorld's killer whales offers an ongoing show of its own. This spot gives the best glimpse of adult whales tending their young.

3 Penguin Encounter
More than 100 knee-high, tuxedo-clad friends from the far north and three species of flighted birds play, swim, and chill in these freezing re-creations of polar seas and snowy banks.

4 Key West Dolphin Fest
Dolphins and false killer whales perform a fantastic series of "behaviors" (formerly called tricks) in this tropical-flavored show, a smaller scale version of SeaWorld's Shamu Adventure show *(see p28)*.

5 Stingray Lagoon
Lean over this waist-high lagoon and pet the velvety hides of stingrays. The ever-hungry rays flock to those offering fish – feeding times are displayed next to the booth selling fish.

6 Dolphin Nursery
When park dolphins give birth, they're brought to this shaded outdoor pool to be with their young calves. Just ask, and the staffer on duty will provide lots of fascinating information.

7 Sky Tower
For a marvellous view of the park and all its backstage areas, take a guided trip to the top of the 450-ft- (137-m) Sky Tower (extra admission fee required).

8 Clydesdales
Take a break from sea creatures and visit the Clydesdale Hamlet to tour the stables of the world-famous Anheuser Busch team of Clydesdale horses. There are plenty of photo opportunities.

9 Shamu's Happy Harbor
Kids can only focus for so long. After that, bring them to this huge play-ground, complete with slides, a mini-waterpark, a four-story maze of nets, steel drums, and a separate sandbox for smaller guests.

10 Cirque de la Mer
This is mostly a confused and shameless rip-off of Cirque du Soleil *(see p89)*. But it is redeemed by the wacky mime antics of Peruvian comic Cesar Aedo, whose audience participation stunts are genuinely funny.

Cirque de la Mer

For information on Discovery Cove, SeaWorld's sister park **See p97**

Top 10 Rescued Animals at SeaWorld Orlando

1 Sea turtles *(Cheloniidae)*
2 Manatees *(Trichechus)*
3 Pygmy sperm whales *(Kogia breviceps)*
4 Dwarf sperm whales *(Kogia simus)*
5 Pilot whales *(Globicephala)*
6 Bottlenose dolphins *(Tursiops truncatus)*
7 Killer whales *(Orcinus orca)*
8 Sandhill cranes *(Grus canadensis)*
9 Herons *(Ardeidae)*
10 Grackles *(Quiscalus)*

SeaWorld's Rescue & Rehabilitation Program

Park staff do more than teach killer whales to splash the audience on command. As part of their commitment to conservation, animal experts at all SeaWorld parks in Orlando, Texas, and California are on call 24 hours a day to rescue sick or injured sea mammals, birds, and turtles. These animals are sheltered at the parks, nursed back to health, and – whenever possible – released into the wild. Endangered Florida manatees are regular bene-ficiaries of the rescue program. As a result of motor-boat propellers, tangled fishing lines, and dangerous toxins, numerous manatees are injured or killed each year. When the call goes out, SeaWorld responds with a specially equipped animal rescue unit, which can begin emergency treatment on the spot. Manatees on the mend, along with those that wouldn't survive in the wild, are housed in the park's Manatee exhibit (see p29). Since SeaWorld Orlando started its rescue program in 1976, it has been responsible for saving more than 270 manatees, with more than 100 released back into the wild. By the end of 2000, SeaWorld Orlando's entire program had rescued and cared for 3,251 animals, including those from animal shelters, and released 735 back into the wild.

Breeding program
SeaWorld also has a hugely successful breeding program: baby penguins, seals, and no less than 10 killer whale calves have been born at SeaWorld Orlando.

SeaWorld staff conducting a triple manatee release

Following pages **Kraken Ride, SeaWorld Orlando**

Wet 'n Wild

Opened in 1977 by George Millay, the founder of SeaWorld, Wet 'n Wild boasts an awesome collection of rides, family activities, and a beach party atmosphere that visitors of all ages enjoy. There is a refreshing lack of merchandise tie-ins here, even though the park is now owned by Universal Studios. The focus is on original thrill rides that leave guests breathless and grinning. Despite strong challenges by Disney World in the form of Blizzard Beach and Typhoon Lagoon, Wet 'n Wild remains the region's best water park, and one of the area's top attractions.

The central Surf Lagoon

🍴 **Bubba's Bar-B-Q & Chicken** is a good bet for lunch. The park's food outlets only accept credit cards or prepaid money wristbands, available at Guest Services.

⚠️ Steps to rides and asphalt walkways can get very hot in high temperatures. Wear non-slip footwear as protection.

Hi-speed rides can leave you uncovered! Ladies, avoid bikinis or consider adding a T-shirt.

Rides have a 36-inch (91-cm) minimum height requirement for kids riding solo.

⊙ *6200 International Dr*
• *Map T2*
• *1-800-992-9453*
• *www.wetnwild.com*
• *Open 10am–5pm daily, call to check seasonal hours • Adm: adults $29.95, children (3–9) $23.95 (plus 6% tax), children under 3 are free. Afternoon discounts are available year-round.*

Top 10 Features

1. Der Stuka/The Bomb Bay
2. The Storm
3. Black Hole
4. Blue Niagara
5. Mach 5
6. The Flyer
7. Lazy River
8. Bubba Tub
9. Bubble Up
10. Hydra Fighter

1 Der Stuka/The Bomb Bay

The park's scariest ride has two options. Der Stuka is a six-story free fall down a 78-degree incline; the steeper Bomb Bay *(below)* is just as high but even more terrifying.

2 The Storm

Hurtle down a shoot filled with mist, thunder, and (at night) lightning, then swirl into an open bowl before dropping into a lower pool. Thrilling.

3 Black Hole

Two people in a raft hang on for dear life as they travel 500 ft (153 m) of twisting tubes in pitch-black darkness *(right)*.

4 Blue Niagara

Two interwoven tubes 300-ft (92-m) long drop riders down six stories into the bracing water of a splash-landing tank.

Mach 5
5 A solo flume navigated by riders on a foam mat. On tight turns, ride the flowing water as far up the wall as possible.

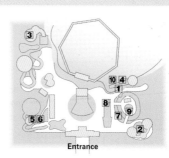

Wet 'n Wild Park Plan

The Flyer
6 On this watery toboggan run, four riders mount one raft and plow through 450 ft (137 m) of banked curves and racing straight runs.

Lazy River
7 A mile-long (1.6-km) circular waterway *(left)*, which gently winds past swaying palms, tropical flowers, and waterfalls. Perfect for slowly floating along in an inner tube (you'll need to rent one), or for a refreshing swim that takes you back to where you started.

Bubba Tub
8 This six story-high slide *(left)* offers three big drops during its descent. The large circular rafts hold up to five, making it perfect for getting the whole family screaming.

Bubble Up
9 A slippery version of the King of the Castle game, for children up to 12 years old. Grab the ropes to try to climb up the large inflated balloon without bouncing off and falling into the 3-ft- (91-cm) deep pool. Water cannons add to the utter chaos – and to the fun.

Hydra Fighter
10 Strapped back-to-back in a swing and armed with water cannons *(above)*, two riders are supposed to create their own ride. But it usually degenerates into a water fight between riders in all of the eight swings!

Park Guide

Wet 'n Wild's aquatic center is the giant Surf Lagoon, which is encircled by various rides. On entering the park, bear right and head to the Tube, Towel & Locker Rental counter to get a locker for your belongings. You can return to it whenever you need to during the day. Guest Services is located on the left as you go into the park. If you plan to do some tanning or lying around, try to reserve a beach chair with your towel before hitting the rides, and make sure you've got sunscreen. After that, just see which ride has the shortest line.

TOP 10 Cypress Gardens

A place of great beauty and unintentional kitsch, Cypress Gardens is the region's oldest continuously running attraction. The gates opened in 1936 and certain things have changed little since; southern belles still stroll the grounds in ante-bellum finery, the gardens continue to impress, and, as ever, the water-ski show wows the crowds. The older set in particular head here for a taste of Florida that's far removed from Disney.

View from the Sky Tower

🟢 Try a slice of key lime pie from the Baker's Dozen to keep you going.

Chalet Suzanne, 10 miles (16 km) from Cypress Gardens, is worth the detour for a special meal: try moon soup (as eaten by astronauts on board Apollo 15 & 16), lump crab, and rum pie. Reserve ahead. (*1-863-676-6011*).

🟢 The Junior Belle Program ($44.95 plus 6% tax) gives girls the opportunity to dress up like a southern belle for two hours.

🌐 *2641 S. Lake Summit Dr, Winter Haven*
• *Off map*
• *1-863-324-2111*
• *www.cypress gardens.com*
• *Open 9:30am–5pm daily (until 8pm or 9pm 1 week in Jan, plus Feb–Apr, Nov & Dec)*
• *Adm: adults $34.95, children (6–12) $19.95 (all plus 6% tax), children under six go free.*
• *Closed Christmas Day.*

Top 10 Attractions

1. Botanical Gardens
2. 2001 Ski Odyssey
3. Botanical Gardens Cruise
4. Wings of Wonder
5. Southern Breeze
6. Calling All Animals
7. Birdwalk Aviary
8. Islands in the Sky
9. Cypress Junction
10. Cypress Roots

2️⃣ 2001 Ski Odyssey
What started as a show for World War II troops is now billed as the "Greatest American Ski Team". Aquamaids, ramp-masters, and a clown perform slightly corny but nevertheless breathtaking acrobatics and stunts.

1️⃣ Botanical Gardens
Seasonal flower festivals *(below)* bring a riot of color as thousands of chrysanthemums (Nov), poinsettias (Dec–Jan), and spring flowers (Mar–May) are planted. There are extraordinary examples of topiary, too.

3️⃣ Botanical Gardens Cruise
When water levels permit, this is a gentle meander along scenic canals and past waving belles who stand against a backdrop of some of the garden's 8,000 varieties of flora.

4️⃣ Wings of Wonder
One thousand butterflies, representing 50 varieties, fly freely in this conservatory. It includes a hatching display where the stages of metamorphosis can be seen.

5 Southern Breeze

For an extra fee, hop aboard this authentic, stern-driven paddle-wheel boat, which takes passengers on a lazy, 40-minute tour of the park and neighboring wetlands.

Cypress Gardens Plan

6 Calling All Animals

A collection of alligators, crocodiles, raptors, a fun-loving coatimundi, a 6-ft (2-m) savanna monitor lizard, and a 15-ft (4-m) albino python (named "Banana Boy") star in this educational and entertaining animal encounter.

7 Birdwalk Aviary

Lories and lorikeets, which have been raised by hand, fly over to beg for a sip of the nectar you can give them in small cups. Some leave a little something on your shoulder to show their gratitude. The aviary also has pheasants, ducks, and small deer.

8 Islands in the Sky

Float 153 ft (47 m) up on this popular sky ride, which offers a wonderful panorama of the gardens, the Chain of Lakes, as well as the countryside that surrounds the park.

9 Cypress Junction

You don't have to love trains to be impressed by this detailed model railroad *(below)*. Twenty trains ply its 1,100 ft (335 m) of track, visiting miniature US landmarks, complete with tiny people and animals.

10 Cypress Roots

This clapboard house plays host to a museum of memorabilia, including photos of Elvis on water skis, plus video and magazine interviews with the Popes, the founders of Cypress Gardens.

Garden guide

The park takes about 45 minutes to get to by car from Orlando. It stretches for 200 acres (81 ha) but it's easy to cover the attractions in one day. Crowds aren't as big as those in Orlando, so the pace is more relaxed. Carousel Cove offers kiddie rides, and the nearby Wacky Waters gives them a chance to cool off. Maps are available at Guest Relations to the right of the entrance.

🔟 Kennedy Space Center

More than any other Florida attraction, the Kennedy Space Center celebrates the fruits of human inquiry and imagination. Owned by the National Aeronautics and Space Administration (NASA), the center was built as a means for astronauts' and employees' families to view center operations. Today, it offers a fascinating window on life beyond Earth to more than 2.2 million visitors each year, and is the site of many dramatic space shuttle launches.

Vehicle Assembly Building

🌭 Grab a hot dog and sit next to a chunk of real moon rock at the Moon Rock Café.

🎟 Special tickets (available up to six weeks before launch dates) allow access to the launch viewing area. Call 1-321-449-4444 for information.

Call Mears Transportation to arrange transport to the center: 407-423-5566.

🛈 Rte 405, Titusville • Off map • 1-321-452-2121 • www.kennedyspace center.com • Open 9am–5:30pm daily. Closed Dec. 25 and Shuttle launch dates • Adm: $25; children (3–11) $15; plus 6% tax. Children under 3 go free. • Shuttle launch tickets: $15; children (0–2) go free; for info on forthcoming lauches check www-pao.ksc.nasa.gov • Call for details of inclusive tour & Center admission tickets.

Top 10 Attractions

1. Shuttle Launches
2. Cape Canaveral: Then & Now Tour
3. Astronaut Memorial
4. Astronaut Encounter
5. LC39 Observation Gantry
6. IMAX Theaters
7. International Space Station Exhibit
8. Saturn/Apollo V Center
9. Rocket Garden
10. Early Space & New Millennium Exhibits

1 Shuttle Launches
The Center closes for part of the day when a shuttle launches, but watching this, the ultimate Florida thrill ride (*below*), is a moving, once-in-a-lifetime experience.

2 Cape Canaveral: Then & Now Tour
This two-hour tour visits attractions including historic launch pads and the US Air Force Space & Missile Museum.

3 Astronaut Memorial
The Center's most sobering exhibit is this massive black granite monument to the 17 US astronauts who gave their lives for space exploration.

4 Astronaut Encounter
Meet a spaceman when astronauts from various space programs visit the Center (*right*). Expect question-and-answer periods, personal stories, video presentations, and space artifacts.

5 LC39 Observation Gantry
Views from this tower include the Vehicle Assembly Building and the Crawlerway Track, an eight-lane highway on which shuttles trundle to the launch pad at 1 mph (1.6 kmph).

IMAGES Theaters
6 The Center's twin, back-to-back, 5.5-story theaters show two films. The 3-D *L5: First City in Space* suggests what the first space colony might be like, while *The Dream Is Alive* is an inspiring, past-to-present feature on the space shuttle program.

Kennedy Space Center Plan

International Space
7 Station Exhibit
Here, visitors can explore detailed, full-scale models of the International Space Station's compartments and see actual components being prepared for use.

Saturn/Apollo V
8 Center
One of only three Saturn V rockets *(see p40)* in existence, footage of the first Moon mission, a lunar module model *(above)*, and other exhibits here re-create the Apollo missions.

Center Guide

About a 45-minute drive from Orlando, the Center forms part of the Merritt Island National Wildlife Refuge *(see p52)*. Admission includes a bus tour to exhibits located away from the Visitor Complex; it's worth renting the tour's audio guide. Boarding areas for the bus tours are to the right of the ticket plaza and information center (where maps are available). Except for launch days, the center is rarely overcrowded.

Rocket Garden
9 Unlike any other garden you have seen, the Kennedy Space Center's contains eight actual rockets, including a Mercury Atlas similar to the one that was used to launch astronaut John Glenn. Special effects create the illusion of the rockets taking off.

Early Space & New Millennium Exhibits
10 These two adjoining exhibits offer passive peeks at the actual Mercury Mission Control consoles used for the first American manned flights, a chance to touch a real Mars rock *(above)*, and the opportunity to submit your name for a future mission.

Left **Saturn V** Center **X-15** Right **Gemini VII capsule lauched by Titan II**

Rockets: Past, Present, & Future

1 Jupiter C
This early variation of the Mercury Redstone rocket *(see below)* was developed by a team headed by the German scientist Wernher von Braun. The Jupiter C carried the USA's first satellite, Explorer I, which launched on January 31, 1958.

2 X-15
The X-15 rocket plane flew 199 missions from 1959 to 1968, carrying a who's who of astronauts, including moon-walker Neil Armstrong. It reached altitudes of 354,200 ft (107,960 m) and speeds of 4,520mph (7,274 kmph).

3 Mercury Redstone
This rocket carried the first American into space. Alan B. Shepard Jr.'s 15-minute, 22-second ride aboard the Freedom 7 capsule in 1961 was one of six flights in the Mercury program.

4 Mercury Atlas
When the six-flight Mercury program graduated from sub-orbital to orbital flights, the Atlas replaced the Mercury Redstone. This rocket took John Glenn, Scott Carpenter, Wally Schirra, and Gordon Cooper into space in 1962–3.

5 Titan II
When a larger capsule was needed for two-person crews, this rocket earned its place in NASA history. It was used for 10 manned flights (Gemini Titan expeditions) in 1965 and 1966.

6 Saturn V
At 363 ft (110 m), this was the largest launch vehicle ever produced. The highlight of its career was Apollo 11, the 8-day, 1969 mission that landed Buzz Aldrin and Neil Armstrong on the moon.

7 Titan Centaur
The Titan Centaur rocket launched Voyager I and II in 1977 on a mission to explore Jupiter and Saturn, Uranus, and, 12 years after its launch, Neptune.

8 Pegasus
Today's version of this winged wonder is less than mythical but more than capable of flying small communications satellites into a low Earth orbit from the bellies of mother ships such as the L-1011.

9 X-43A Launch Vehicle
These diminutive rockets may one day boost small, unmanned jets at high speeds and altitudes, improving the safety of manned flights.

10 X-34 Rocketplane
Welcome to the future? NASA's reusable rocket plane will look like a small space shuttle and will be able to fly at twice the speed of the X-15. However, budget cuts could mean it doesn't get off the ground at all.

Mercury Redstone

Top 10 US Manned Space Program Events

1. **May 5, 1961** Alan B. Shepard, Jr. becomes the first American in space.
2. **Feb 20, 1962** John H. Glenn, Jr. becomes the first American to orbit the Earth.
3. **Jun 3, 1965** Edward H. White, Jr. becomes the first American to walk in space.
4. **Jan 27, 1967** Gus Grissom and two other astronauts die in a test launch fire.
5. **Jul 20, 1969** Neil A. Armstrong becomes the first person to walk on the moon.
6. **Apr 11–13, 1970** An explosion nearly causes disaster for Apollo 13.
7. **Apr 12, 1981** The first Shuttle is launched.
8. **Jan 28, 1986** Seven astronauts die in the Challenger space shuttle explosion.
9. **Jun 27–Jul 7, 1995** US astronauts first dock on the Russian space station Mir.
10. **May 27–Jun 6, 1999** The space shuttle docks for the first time on the International Space Station.

The Space Shuttle

Due to their current and ongoing role in the space program, space shuttles (of which there are four) are the best recognized of NASA's vehicles, venturing into space with names like Discovery and Endeavor. The latter replaced the Challenger shuttle which exploded on the shuttles' 51st mission (January 28, 1986) just 73 seconds after launch, killing all seven crew members. After a two-year hiatus for safety checks, the shuttle program resumed with renewed vigor. Once in orbit, each is capable of cruising at 17,500 mph (28,163 kmph) – some 300 times faster than an average US road cruising speed of 55 mph (88 kmph) – and their cargo bays can hold a fully loaded tour bus. Yet the engineless orbiter can glide to a runway more gracefully than a pelican landing on water.

The 100th Space Shuttle launch

Investigations in Space

The shuttles allow astronauts to conduct a wide range of experiments. Here, mission specialist Kathryn P. Hire undergoes a sleep study experiment in the Neurolab on board the Earth-orbiting Space Shuttle Columbia (April 20, 1998).

41

Left **Dueling Dragons** Right **Incredible Hulk Roller Coaster, both Islands of Adventure**

Thrill Rides

1 Splash Mountain
Prepare to get wet on this deep-drop ride unless you wear protective clothing. In summer, it's a cooling trip; at any time of year it's one to enjoy as a spectator from the bridge between Frontierland and Adventureland. Even in that relative safety you may get drenched. See p8 (Magic Kingdom).

2 Twilight Zone Tower of Terror
This is one of the rides thrill junkies rent (at a price) for their own private parties. You can have just as much fun without the premium, though be warned this ride's mechanisms sometimes develop minor glitches, causing heads to knock on the ceiling as riders plunge back to sea level. See p16 (Disney-MGM Studios).

3 Rock 'n' Roller Coaster
This ride accelerates like a military jet. If that isn't enough to make heads spin, each 24-passenger "stretch limo" has 120 speakers that blare Aerosmith hits at a teeth-rattling decibel level. See p16 (Disney-MGM Studios).

4 Incredible Hulk Coaster
Possibly the ultimate inversion ride – it's a zero-G-force, multi-looping ride of a lifetime. The net catches personal items riders should have stashed in a locker. See p20 (Islands of Adventure).

5 Dueling Dragons
The ride climbs 12.5 stories above the ground before you realize it's too late and you're locked in for the duration. To increase the adrenaline rush, try to get one of the two outside seats in the first eight rows of either dragon. Centrifugal force will steal some of your courage. See p20 (Islands of Adventure).

Dr Doom's Fearfall

6 The Amazing Adventures of Spider-Man
More high-tech than Universal Studios' Back to the Future, but tamer than the Dragon and Hulk coasters. Still, it's not for those with heart problems or motion sickness tendencies. Use the single line if alone or can split from your group – it's quicker. See p20 (Islands of Adventure).

7 Doctor Doom's Fearfall
This is a bit like free-falling in a metal harness. As your legs dangle free and you bob to a

Kraken, Islands of Adventure

Many thrill rides are not suitable for young children.

stop, you'll probably be screaming at the top of your lungs.
See p20 (Islands of Adventure).

8 Dudley Do-Right's Ripsaw Falls

Dudley can be very deceptive – it
looks pretty harmless, but this ride
has a big dip where, thanks to
some smoke and mirrors, it feels
like you've plunged 20 ft (6 m) or
so under the surface of the water.
See p20 (Islands of Adventure).

9 Kraken

Think pure speed as
Poseidon's mythological underwater beast breaks free and
without warning pulls your 32-
passenger train 151 ft (46 m)
closer to heaven, then dives
144 ft (44 m) back toward hell at
speeds of 65 mph (104 kmph)!
If you survive, expect seven loops
on a 4,177-ft (1,273-m) course.
This may just be the longest 3
minutes, 39 seconds of your
existence. *See p28 (SeaWorld).*

10 Summit Plummet

No water park ride will tangle
up your bathing suit faster than
this 120-ft (36-m), partial-dark-
ness ride. It starts slow, but ends
in a near vertical drop that has you
plummeting at 60 mph (96 kmph).
It's not for the weak of heart or
those under 48 inches (122 cm).
See p89 (Blizzard Beach).

Top 10 Thrill Rides for Children

1 The Barnstormer at Goofy's Wiseacre Farm
This ton-of-fun kid-size roller
coaster is a breath-stopping,
60-second ride. *See p8.*

2 Cinderella's Golden Carrousel
A 100-year-old beauty with an
engaging fairy-tale theme.
See p9.

3 The Many Adventures of Winnie the Pooh
Pooh created controversy
when he replaced Mr. Toad's
Wild Ride in 1999, but he's
since won converts. *See p9.*

4 Magic Carpets of Aladdin
This gentle ride is Adventureland's first new attraction in
30 years. *See p9.*

5 Flying Unicorn
Like the Barnstormer and
Woody's Nuthouse, this one's
corkscrew action is a blast.
See p22.

6 Pteranodon Flyers
A neat aerial adventure,
but it can make some riders
queasy. *See p20.*

7 The Cat in the Hat
This ride's dizzying, 24-ft
(7-m) tunnel can leave your
head and tummy in a spin.
See p21.

8 Caro-Seuss-El
Seussian characters make
this carousel ride truly unique.
See p22.

9 E.T. Adventure
You may have to wait in line
a while before pedaling your
bicycle past fantastic scenery
and characters. *See p26.*

10 Woody Woodpecker's Nuthouse Coaster
The banked turns of this
mini coaster are absolutely
exhilarating. *See p26.*

For more on minimum height requirements **See p139**

43

Left **Titanic – Ship of Dreams** Right **Ripley's Believe It Or Not! Odditorium**

Smaller Attractions

1 Gatorland
This park, which recently turned 50, is chock-full of around 800 lurking alligators, honking for mates, and sometimes performing tricks. The gators don't sit up and beg, but they do jump for food – raw chicken, to be exact, dangled over their ponds by a brave employee. Two hundred or so crocodiles are here to add diversity, as are snakes and other reptiles. The gator-wrestling show is an impressive must-see. *See p107.*

2 The Holy Land Experience
Ancient Jerusalem comes to life at this attraction, which has reconstructions of Jesus' tomb, the temple, and the caves where the Dead Sea scrolls were found. Make no mistake: this is a "Christ-centered ministry," but guests of any religion can get a kick out of cast members acting out biblical scenes and telling stories from both testaments. A café serves up "Goliath burgers" among other fare. *See p98.*

3 Ripley's Believe It or Not! Odditorium
Cunningly designed, this building looks like it's about to slip into the ground. Inside, kids might squeal – and adults might cringe – over the replicas of human and animal oddities on display. Two-headed cat, anyone? A movie shows people swallowing coat hangers, light bulbs, and more. There are also plenty of quirky displays, such as a rendition of the *Mona Lisa* made out of toast. *See p98.*

4 Titanic – Ship of Dreams
The spirit of Leo DiCaprio lingers around this impressive recreation of the doomed Titanic. Guided tours by actors playing crew members and passengers bring the displays to life. Among the 200 or so exhibits are life jackets salvaged from the ship, which add a solemn touch. *See p99.*

5 Fun Spot Action Park
Looking for life in the fast lane? The Fun Spot's four giant go-kart tracks allow you to "vroom" at your own speed, buzzing around corkscrew turns to the finish line. There are also bumper cars and boats, a huge ferris wheel, and an arcade full of simulators to round off the package.
⊗ *5551 Del Verde Way • Map E3 • Open noon–midnight Mon-Fri, 10am–midnight Sat–Sun • Adm*

Gatorland

6 Splendid China

Scaled-down attractions from the world's most populous country are the draw at Splendid China. Here, the top of the Great Wall is at eye level – but it's still a half-mile (1-km) long. Wander the Forbidden City, walk through the Tomb of Terracotta Warriors, and marvel at the flexible acrobats in a live show. The Suzhou Gardens area is a wonderful reconstruction of China's Suzhou town as it would have looked 700 years ago, complete with pagoda. *See p108.*

Splendid China

7 A World of Orchids

Orchids come in a multitude of strange shapes and colors, all of which are on display at this working greenhouse, home to 1,000 of the exotic flowers. Lush paths, serene streams, and the occasional squawk from a parrot offer respite from the busy hub-bub of the theme parks. *See p107.*

8 WonderWorks

Gimmicks abound inside this building, which, like Ripley's, is sinking into the ground, only this time it's roof first. Inside, there's an interactive arcade of some mild scientific educational value. Among the more than 85 hands-on activities, the curious can experience an earthquake or virtual hang gliding, and test their reflexes. For simple fun, the huge laser-tag field is a blast. *See p99.*

9 Jungleland Zoo

Originally an animal refuge, this is a small, old-time zoo that still has cages rather than natural habitats. The charm comes from the up-close experience of exotic animals, including plenty of big cats and monkeys. Jungleland is marked by a big, gaping fiberglass alligator out front; inside, attractions include gator-wrestling and a more docile petting zoo. ◎ *4580 W. Hwy 192, Kissimmee • Map H3 • Open 9am– 6pm daily • Adm*

10 Winter Park Scenic Boat Tour

Glide through three of Winter Park's lakes on a pontoon boat for this hour-long tour. Nature-lovers can spot birds such as ospreys and herons. The more material-istic can swoon over huge lake-side mansions, sometimes getting close enough to peek in a window. The architecture of Rollins College, and the secluded feel of the canals, make this tour a popular option for the kitsch-weary. *See p119.*

Left **Swan Boats, Lake Eola** Right **Citywalk**

TOP 10 Ways to Have Fun on the Cheap

1 The Peabody Ducks
It all began in the 1930s when a couple of inebriated sportsmen returning from a week-end hunting trip thought it would be funny to put live ducks in the Peabody Hotel's lobby fountain. The joke stuck and now the original ducks' descendants are local celebrities. They march down from their penthouse at 11am, via the elevator, and return at 5pm. ✪ *9801 International Dr • Map T4 • Free*

2 HOB Blues Bar
The main room at House of Blues is one of the best spots in town to catch big-name acts *(see p74)*. But the HOB Blues Bar, next door, is an intimate stage for small-scale blues bands that are generally unknown but excellent. Guests ordering dinner get priority for table seating. ✪ *Downtown Disney Westside • Map G2 • Open 11am–11.30pm Sun–Wed (to 1:30am Thu–Sat) • Free*

The Peabody Ducks

3 Kissimmee Rodeo
Every Friday night, cowboys (and girls) from all over the Southeast mosey over to Kissimmee for an evening of calf roping, bareback riding, barrel racing, bull riding, and more. Unusually for Orlando, this is not an attraction but a genuine rodeo competition, with cash prizes. The action is live, unrehearsed, and, for those who've never seen the real thing before, quite something. A cheap and eventful evening out. *See p109.*

4 Downtown Disney
With three parts – Westside, Pleasure Island, and Marketplace – glittering Downtown Disney has become the epicenter of nightlife at "the Mouse". Although Pleasure Island and its nightclubs boast the most obvious party appeal, both Westside and Marketplace are also packed day and night. Hordes of guests (especially families) stroll among the area's shops and restaurants – it's bustling, fun, and costs little to enjoy. Kids in particular like the LEGO Store's *(see p92)* outdoor work stations. *See p67.*

5 Disney's BoardWalk
Almost an accidental attraction, this is a re-creation of a 1940s seaside resort, complete with street performers, carnival games, great restaurants and bars. The ESPN Club is the perfect spot to draw on a beer and catch a major-league game on big-screen TVs. *See p93.*

6 Center for Birds of Prey

Founded by the Florida Audubon Society, and off the beaten tourist track, this center's primary function is to rescue and rehabilitate wounded and orphaned raptors. Birds of prey that can't be released back into the wild, however, are kept and used to educate the public about wildlife conservation. With knowledgeable staff and the opportunity to stand close to birds such as eagles and vultures, the center is a captivating treat for a handful of dollars. *See p120.*

Kissimmee Rodeo

7 Universal's CityWalk & Portofino Bay Boat Ride

By day, visitors stroll through this area of restaurants and shops on their way to Universal Studios and Islands of Adventure *(see pp20–27)*. In the evening, CityWalk becomes it's own sparkling destination, a swinging Downtown with outdoor entertainment and pulsating crowds to rival Disney's BoardWalk. For 15 minutes of quiet romance, take the free boat ride (which runs until 2am) between CityWalk and the Portofino Bay Hotel *(see p142)*. In the moonlight, the Portofino's *faux* Italian paint job looks even more convincing. ◈ *Map T1*

8 Swan Boats In Lake Eola

Tucked under the blossoming skyline of downtown Orlando, Lake Eola Park is a charming city oasis *(see p52)*. Those seeking some (inexpensive) time alone can rent a two-person Swan Boat (propelled by pedal power) and cruise about on the lake. *See p114.*

9 Fort Wilderness Petting Farm

For kids who want to ride a pony (for a small charge) or get to pet miniature donkeys, goats, and other farmyard creatures, this splendid little park can't be beaten. ◈ *Walt Disney World • Map F2 • Open 10am–5pm daily • Free*

10 Orlando Speedworld Speedway

This racetrack, 17 miles (30 km) east of Orlando, sees eight divisions of highly modified stock cars race each week. However, the most entertaining evenings are those featuring destructive, madcap races like Schoolbus Demolition Derbys, and Boat and Trailer Races. The price depends on what's on, but it's always a cheap night out. ◈ *Highway 50 (at the 520 Cocoa cutoff), Bithlo • Map F1 • 407-568-1367 • Open from 8pm Fri. • Adm*

Left **Wet 'n Wild** Right **Discovery Cove**

🔟 Places to Cool Off

1 Wet 'n Wild
Orlando's best water park is full of rides and slides to keep the most hardened thrill-seeker's adrenalin pumping. But it's not all action – there are kids' rides and chill-out areas, too. *See pp34–5.*

2 Discovery Cove
Need to unwind on a tropical beach, swim with dolphins, or snorkel over coral reefs? Well, if you check into Discovery Cove, you can. This exclusive (daily entry is limited to 1,000 people) and inspired Orlando attraction offers the features and personalized services of an upscale island resort. Admission is not cheap, but includes everything from lunch to wet suits and sun block. Reservations two months in advance are suggested. *See p97.*

Water Mania

3 Blizzard Beach
In the battle for water park supremacy, Wet 'n Wild's main competitor is this sizeable Disney park. It's what a ski resort would be like if it started to melt, with water slides replacing ski runs. Geared to teens and young adults, the park offers seven water slides and excellent rides, a wave pool, and kids' areas. If park capacity is reached early (as it often is), it closes to new admissions until later in the day. *See p89.*

4 Water Mania
Though not as large as Wet 'n Wild, this Kissimmee park offers a good assortment of slides and thrill rides. Some are unique, such as Wipe Out, a wave generator pool for surfing on body boards, and the Double Berzerker, a steep, double-dip slide. There are also loads of land-based activities such as a children's playground, beach volleyball, and mini-golf. Water Mania often gets packed. *See p106.*

5 Typhoon Lagoon
This Disney water park is an enthralling mix of slides, tubes, and the largest wave pool in the US It's well suited to families with pre-teen children, who'll appreciate the gentler nature of the attractions here. One stand-out is Shark Reef, a short snorkel course over a coral reef teaming with tropical fish and live sharks. Wannabe surfers *(see p57)* can pay an extra fee to use the wave pool out of regular hours. *See p89.*

6 River Country
Huck Finn's old swimming hole is given an update at Disney's third water park. River Country is an aquatic lakeside playground with water slides, swings, and more. It is perfect for families with young kids since

there's nothing too crazy here and there's plenty of room for the little ones to play while Mom or Dad snooze on the beach. The Fort Wilderness Resort location is a short bus ride from the parking area. See p89.

7 Sammy Duvall's Watersports Centers

These Disney World-based centers were founded by four-time world champion water-skier Sammy Duvall. The Contemporary Resort branch offers parasailing, water-skiing, wake-boarding, knee-boarding, and tubing. Guests can either rent a boat and driver or take lessons. The Caribbean Beach Resort one, with its slalom course, is geared to more hardcore water-skiers. Guests can bring their own gear or rent it. § *Map F1 & G2 • Open winter: 10am–5pm daily; summer: 9am–6pm daily • Adm*

8 Buena Vista Watersports

Home to Dave's Ski School, this friendly facility offers water-ski lessons, water-ski and wake-board charters, and rentals of personal watercraft (such as Waverunners and Seaddoos). Perched on the shores of Lake Bryan, Buena Vista Watersports is geared to the beginner, and kids as young as three can join in. Non-skiers and spectators can use the lakeside beach, volleyball net, and picnic area. § *13245 Lake Bryan Rd • Map G3 • Open 9.30am–6pm daily (weather permitting) • Adm*

9 YMCA Aquatic Center

Lap swimmers who find hotel pools insufficient for training will delight in

Jet skiers, Buena Vista Watersports

this championship facility, with its 25-lane regulation lap pool. Although YMCAs are very family-friendly, the facilities here are geared toward serious swimmers. § *8422 International Dr • Map T3 • Adm*

10 Kissimmee Family Aquatic Center

On the eastern edge of Kissimmee, this center offers three pools – one for laps, one for kids, and another for the water slide. It's perfect for families with toddlers or youngsters for whom a major water park could be a bit overwhelming (and admission is far cheaper). § *2204 Denn John Lane • Map H4 • 407-870-7665 • Open Tue–Sat Mar–Sep (times vary) • Adm*

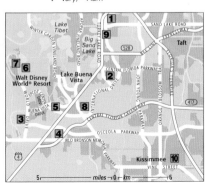

Following Pages **Discovery Cove**

Left **Canaveral National Seashore** Right **Turkey Lake Park**

🔟 Parks & Preserves

1 Canaveral National Seashore & Merritt Island National Wildlife Refuge

These two federal preserves border the Kennedy Space Center and provide habitats for scores of species, including a number of endangered ones, such as sea turtles, manatees, dolphins, alligators, bald eagles, and ospreys. Explore Canaveral's beaches (including a naturist one, Playalinda) and Merritt Island's trails, driving route, and observation deck. 🚫 *Titusville • Off map • Seashore open at least 6am–6pm daily; refuge open at least 9am–5pm daily • Adm (seashore), free (refuge)*

Lake Eola Park

2 Lake Eola Park

Burn a few calories on the 0.9-mile (1.4-km) trail that circles the lake here. Less energetic pursuits include feeding the birds and cruising Lake Eola in the swan-shaped rental boats *(see p47)*. This municipal park is also home to several annual and seasonal events, including the 4th of July fireworks show and the UCF-Shakespeare Festival *(see p64)*. See p114.

3 Wekiva Springs State Park

These springs and the river they feed provide a fertile habitat for such species as white-tail deer, gray foxes, bobcats, raccoons, and black bears. They also provide some of the best places for paddling in a boat in central Florida. With picnic, grilling, camping, and volleyball areas, as well as canoe rentals, this is outdoors heaven. 🚫 *1800 Wekiwa Circle, Apopka • Map A3 • Open 8am–sunset • Adm*

4 Lake Louisa State Park

You can fish (for bass and bream), swim, or paddle a canoe, but you'll have to bring your own equipment. The beach has a bathhouse with showers, and there's a picnic area. White-tail deer, wild turkeys, marsh rabbits, opossums, and raccoons are commonly seen, but don't be surprised if a polecat (also known as a skunk!) cuts across your path. 🚫 *State Park Drive, Clermont • Off map • Open 8am–sunset • Adm*

5 Lake Kissimmee State Park

This is the third largest lake in Florida, which is why the park is one of the best bird-watching areas in the state. You might see bald eagles, and snail kites, as well as whooping and sandhill cranes. On the mammal side, residents include otters, wild turkeys, deer, and fox squirrels. On weekends, the park has a re-created 1876 cattle camp. 🚫 *Camp Mack Rd, Lake Wales • Off map • Open 8am–sunset • Adm*

6 Turkey Lake Park

Unlike many state parks, with natural and usually spartan amenities, this 300-acre (120-ha) city retreat has a swimming pool, picnic pavilions, a lake stocked with fish, three children's playgrounds, nature and jogging trails, and a farm-animal petting zoo. It also has an ecology center, and camping areas if the call of the wild is too strong to leave. ✆ 3401 S. Hiawassee Rd. • Map D3 • Open 7.30am–5pm daily (to 7pm Apr–Oct) • Adm

7 Big Tree Park

The main pull here is the Senator, a 3,500-year-old bald cypress tree, a testament to the life-giving virtues of Central Florida's swamps. It is 17 ft (5 m) in diameter, 47 ft (14 m) in circumference and 125 ft (38 m) tall. The park has picnic tables and a boardwalk through the cypress swamp. ✆ General Hutchison Pkwy, Longwood • Off map • Open 8am–sunset • Free

Wekiva Springs State Park

8 Tosohatchee State Reserve

Swamps dotted with hardwood hammocks (tree islands) and a 19-mile (30-km) stretch of the St. John's River combine to make this one of Central Florida's prettiest and most primitive parks. Photographers will appreciate the scenic locales, some with wild orchids and other flora. Hawks, eagles, fox squirrels, and songbirds can sometimes be seen from the park's trails. ✆ Christmas, 18 miles (29 km) NE of Orlando • Off map • Open 8am– sunset • Adm

9 Wheatley Park

This city park is more urban oasis than rustic countryside retreat. It features lots of facilities such as basketball, tennis, and sand volleyball courts, and picnic areas with grills for a barbecue. Kids will appreciate the well-equipped playground. ✆ 445 W. 13th St, Apopka • Off map • Open sunrise–sunset • Free

10 Ralph V. Chisolm Park

This shady park, on the shore of East Lake Tohopekaliga, has various amenities including a beach, swimming area, horse trails, children's playground, softball and baseball fields, sand volleyball courts, and picnic pavilions. Bring your own equipment, food, and drinks. ✆ 4700 Chisolm Park Trail, St. Cloud • Off map • Open sunrise–sunset • Free

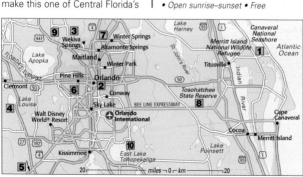

For more on day trips out of the city See pp82–5

53

Left **Clubhouse, Champions Gate** Right **Falcon's Fire**

Golf Courses

1 Disney's Osprey Ridge

Arguably the most challenging of Disney's five 18-hole courses, Osprey Ridge features native woodlands, elevated tees, fairly large greens, nine water holes, and more than 70 bunkers. *Golf Digest's* "Places to Play" ranks it among Florida's best public and resort courses. (Max yds: 7,101 [6,493 m]. USGA rating: 73.9.) ✆ *Golf View Dr • Map F2 • 407-939-4653*

2 Grand Cypress Golf Club

Jack Nicklaus designed these highly rated 45 holes; the New Course was actually inspired by the Old Course at St. Andrews in Scotland. The club is semi-private but has some public tee times available. (Max yds: 6,906 [6,315 m]. USGA rating: 74.4.) ✆ *1 Jacaranda Blvd • Map F2 • 407-239-1909*

3 Disney's Eagle Pines

Pete Dye's Disney design challenges even the best golfers, with dish-shaped fairways, large sand traps, and pine straw rather than grass in the roughs. Sixteen of the 18 holes have water hazards, due in part to the natural wetlands which line this course. (Max yds: 6,772 [6,192 m]. USGA rating: 72.3.) ✆ *Golf View Dr • Map F2 • 407-939-4653*

4 Disney's Magnolia

Here's a course with forgivingly wide fairways that let you hammer the ball. But don't get reckless: 11 of the 18 holes contain water and the course has 97 bunkers, with many waiting to gobble your miss hits. Part of the PGA's National Car Rental Golf Classic *(see p57)* is played here. (Max yds: 7,190 [6,574 m]. USGA rating: 73.9.) ✆ *Palm Dr • Map F1 • 407-939-4653 • Lessons available*

5 Celebration Golf Club

The father-and-son team of Robert Trent Jones, Sr. and Jr. came up with a course that has water on 17 of 18 holes thanks to natural wetlands, so bring an extra ration of balls. There's also a three-hole junior course for 5- to 9-year-olds. (Max yds: 6,786 [6,205 m]. USGA rating: 73.) ✆ *701 Golf Park Dr • Map G2 • 407-566-4653 • Lessons available*

6 Champions Gate

Greg Norman created two 18-hole courses (the National and the International) located in this resort

Villas of Grand Cypress

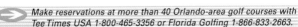

Make reservations at more than 40 Orlando-area golf courses with Tee Times USA 1-800-465-3356 or Florida Golfing 1-866-833-2663.

community southwest of Disney, featuring a terrain of woods, wetlands, and open land. Between them they have 13 water holes, and share double greens at the 4th and 16th holes. (Max yds: 7,048 [6,445 m] and 7,407 [6,773 m], respectively. USGA rating: 75.1 & 76.3.) Ⓢ 1400 Masters Blvd • Map H1 • 407-787-4653 • Lessons available

Orlando Area Golf Course

7 Orange County National – Panther Lake

The elevation changes as much as 60 ft (18 m) in places on this 18-hole course, one of *Golf Digest's* top "Places to Play". It also gets high marks for course condition and pace of play. The course is surrounded by woodlands, while adjoining wetlands and lakes yield 13 water holes. (Max yds: 7,295 [6,670 m]. USGA rating: 75.7.) Ⓢ 16301 Phil Ritson Way • Map E1 • 407-656-2626 • Lessons available

8 Disney's Palm

This jewel of a course is surrounded by woodlands. Half of its holes have water, and its 94 bunkers create headaches for those whose shots stray. The 18th hole is one of the toughest on the PGA Tour. (Max yds: 6,957 [6,391 m]. USGA rating: 73.) Ⓢ Palm Dr • Map F1 • 407-939-4653 • Lessons available

9 Disney's Lake Buena Vista

This tight course with its heavily bunkered fairways and greens also uses dense pine forest to challenge golfers' accuracy. Its most unusual feature is an island green on the seventh hole. Perennially rated as one of Florida's Top 20 in *Golfweek*. (Max yds: 6,819 [6,325 m]. USGA rating: 72.7.) Ⓢ Buena Vista Dr • Map F2 • 407-939-4653

10 Falcon's Fire

With just three water holes, the first nine may convince you to let your guard down, but seven of the last nine holes give you a chance to submerge a ball in two large lakes. This Rees Jones course opened in 1993 and hosts the Senior PGA Tour's qualifying school. (Max yds: 6,901 [6,310 m]. USGA rating: 72.5.) See p110.

Left **Playing tennis, Grand Cypress Raquet Club** Right **Cycling along scenic country trails**

Sports & Outdoor Activities

1 Horseback Riding
Saddle up for 45-minute trail rides at Grand Cypress Resort's state-of-the-art equestrian center. There are horses suitable for all abilities of rider, and lessons are available in either Western or English riding styles. ⊗ *1 N. Jacaranda • Map F2 • 407-239-1938 • Open 9am–5pm daily • Adm*

Trail riding, Grand Cypress Resort

2 Tennis
Disney's Contemporary Resort has six clay courts and its Grand Floridian Resort & Spa has two. The nearby Grand Cypress Raquet Club has 12 courts, including four all-weather ones. ⊗ *Disney • Map F1 • 407-824-2270 • Open 9am–10pm daily • Adm* ⊗ *Grand Cypress • One Hyatt Blvd • Map F2 • 407-239-1944 • Open 9am–10pm daily • Adm*

3 Cycling
Get away from it all on Disney's scenic bike trails. You can rent single, multi-speed, and kids' bikes at the Fort Wilderness Resort's Bike Barn. Tandems and cycles with baby seats and training wheels are also available. ⊗ *Walt Disney World • Map F2 • Open at least 9am–5pm daily • Adm*

4 NFL Experience
No matter if you're out of shape or have never caught a forward pass. At Disney's Wide World of Sports, you can be a gridiron star for the day and take part in a program designed to make you an American football hero – minus the bruises and bleeding. ⊗ *Walt Disney World • Map G2 • Open 9:30am–5pm daily • Adm*

5 Swimming
Most of Orlando's hotels have their own pools, but for a change of scene and a place to swim serious lengths, try an aquatic center. *See p49.*

6 Boating
The man-made lakes around Walt Disney World are perfect for idling away an afternoon. Several of the resorts have small motorboats and pontoon boats for hire. There are also paddle-boats for people who like a more rigorous work-out. ⊗ *Map F1–G2 • Open at least 9am–5pm daily • Adm*

7 Watersports
Test your water-skiing legs at one of Sammy Duvall's Water Sports Centers (which also offers parasailing and wake-boarding). Buena Vista Watersports (which also charters and rents boats) is another option. *See p49.*

Surfing

8 In land-locked Orlando? You bet. According to the state's surf addicts, who sometimes rent the park after hours, Disney's Typhoon Lagoon *(see p48)* has wave-making down to a fine art. But you don't have to be a pro to give it a try. Carroll's Cocoa Beach Surfing School puts on a twice-weekly class for beginners. ✆ *Walt Disney World • Map G2 • 407-939-7529 • Open 6:45–9:30am Tue & Fri • Adm*

Fishing

9 Land your dinner (and a fish story) with Pro Bass Guide Service, a Winter Garden outfit that specializes in guided bass-fishing. Local and regional trips to some of Central Florida's most picturesque rivers and lakes are on offer (pick-up can be arranged), as are offshore expeditions for saltwater species, such as redfish and sea trout. Hotel pickup is available. ✆ *407-877-9636 • Open daily • Adm*

Freshwater fishing, Central Florida

Hayrides

10 For something a little more unusual in the way of outdoor fun, try a 45-minute hay wagon ride around Disney's Fort Wilderness Resort. Expect some singing and dancing, and a good-time atmosphere that makes for a relaxing end to the day. One of Disney's most popular campground experiences. ✆ *Walt Disney World • Map G2 • evenings daily • Adm*

Sporting Events

1 **Florida Citrus Bowl**
The annual college football showdown between the No. 2-ranked teams from the Southeastern and Big Ten conferences. ✆ 407-423-2476 • Jan 1

2 **Walt Disney World Marathon**
A 26.2-mile (42.6-km) race attracting entrants from around the world. ✆ 407-824-4321 • Early Jan

3 **Speedweeks**
Two weeks of motor action at Daytona Beach, ending with the Daytona 500. ✆ 1-386-253-7223 • Early Feb

4 **Silver Spurs Rodeo**
Two days of rodeo events for cowboys and girls in Kissimmee. ✆ 407-847-5118 • Third weekend in Feb

5 **Bay Hill Invitational**
Golf legend host, Arnie Palmer, plus players like Tiger Woods are the draw. ✆ 407-876-2429 • Mid-Mar

6 **Atlanta Braves Spring Training**
Catch baseball's Braves in pre-season training. ✆ 407-828-3267 • Mar

7 **Orlando Predators**
Grab a chance to support the local football team. ✆ 407-447-7337 • Apr–Aug

8 **Orlando Miracle**
See the women's basketball team in action. ✆ 407-916-9622 • Jun–Sep

9 **Orlando Magic**
Don't miss the NBA team if it's the season. ✆ 407-896-2442 • Oct–Apr

10 **National Car Rental Golf Classic**
Disney hosts a multitude of tour professionals in a week of golfing events. ✆ 407-824-4321 • Mid-Oct

For more Orlando area events See pp64–5

Left **Spa at Renaissance Orlando Resort** Right **Massage Works Day Spa & Fitness**

TOP 10 Spas

1 Spa at the Wyndham Palace Resort

Just around the corner from Disney's parks, the Wyndham offers an upscale experience that's from another world. This full-service, European-style spa has various styles of massage; body treatments (mud masks, wraps, and polishes); facials; and hydrotherapy treatments. It has steam rooms, saunas, and a health-and-fitness center. ✪ 1900 Buena Vista Dr • Map G2 • 407-827-3200 • Usually open 9am–6pm daily

2 Greenhouse Spa at the Portofino Bay Hotel

A state-of-the-art fitness center with a full-service spa (massages, saunas, facials, a couple's treatment room, and more) are on offer at this Universal resort. If you are a guest, you can choose to have your massage in your room. ✪ 5601 Universal Blvd • Map T1 • 407-503-1000 • Open 9am-6pm daily

3 Grand Floridian Spa & Health Club

The spa at Disney's Victorian-style resort has a whole range of services including water and massage therapies, aromatherapy, body wraps, and masks. There's a couple's treatment room and a well-equipped health club. The Grand Floridian also offers

Urban Spa at Eó Inn

nutrition and fitness counseling. ✪ 4401 Floridian Way • Map F1 • 407-824-2332 • Open 8am–8pm daily

4 Serenity Salon & Day Spa

This popular day spa is a nice alternative to the resort spas. It's a little less expensive, but it's also some way north of the tourist areas. Treatments range from massages (Swedish, prenatal and four-hand) and facials to more decadent services, such as milk-and-wine salt scrubs and mud body wraps. ✪ 2401 W. State Rd 434 • Off map • 407-788-8585 • Open at least 9am–5pm daily

5 Spa at Renaissance Orlando Resort

This spa features a full line of traditional services including massages (Swedish, deep tissue, and reflexology); body treatments (polishes and wraps); and a full line of facials, one of which is designed to introduce 10- to 14-year-olds to the basics of skin care. In-room massages are available for an extra charge. The fitness center has modern Nautilus equipment. ✪ 6677 Sea Harbor Dr • Map T5 • 407-351-5555 • Open 8am–8pm

6 Spa at the Disney Institute

Once a regular Disney resort, the Institute is now a corporate-client-only affair, but its spa and fitness center remain open to the public. Treatments include seaweed and sea-foam mud wraps, deep-pore cleansing, and French body polishes as well as various massages and facials (seaweed, replenishing, and men's). There's a fitness center, too. ❀ *1920 Magnolia Dr • Map G2 • 407-827-4455 • Open 8am–5pm, sometimes later*

7 Le Spa de Moor

Located north of Orlando, Kathy Nicholson and her small staff offer a diverse menu that includes cellulite and detoxifying body wraps, aromatherapy treatments, mineralizing body buffs, French foot treatments, and body masks. There's also a full line of massages as well as six-hour, multi-service packages. ❀ *1240 Fairview Ave • Map L2 • 407-740-5288 • Open 9am–9pm Mon–Sat*

8 Urban Spa at Eó Inn

This is a funky spa in a downtown boutique hotel *(see p144)*. Headliners include soothing Swedish, deep tissue, and Shiatsu massages; body waxes; seaweed or mud wraps; European, hydrointensive, and men's facials; seasalt scrubs; and a full-line of salon services. Packages combine your choice of three to five services. ❀ *227 N. Eola Dr • Map P3 • 407-481-8485 • Open 9am–6pm daily*

9 Massageworks Day Spa & Fitness

Located in a 100-year-old Kissimmee schoolhouse, this spa has an air of yesteryear. Treatments include massages (Swedish, neuromuscular, reflexology, and sports); therapies (salt scrubs, aroma steam, and mud-aloe); wraps (oil, marine algae, and sea clay); and colonic irrigation. Yoga, kick-boxing, and martial arts are also on offer, and there's a sauna.

Spa at the Wyndham Palace Resort

It's possible to combine treatments in three- to six-hour packages. ❀ *405 Church St • Map P2 • 407-932-0300 • Open 8am–7pm Mon–Sat*

10 Suzzann David Salon Day Spa

It's around a 30-minute drive from downtown Orlando, but if you're mobile, or staying in the north of the city, your reward is a soothing retreat. Services include massages (Swedish, prenatal, and aromatherapy); body wraps (mud, seaweed, and heat); and facials (European and anti-oxidant). ❀ *120 International Pkwy • Off map • 407-333-3571 • Open 9am–8pm Tue–Fri; 9am–5pm Sat*

Left **Exhibit, Mennello Museum of American Folk Art** Right **Orlando Science Center**

TOP10 Museums

1 Orlando Museum of Art

Following a multi-million dollar makeover in 1997, the Orlando Museum of Art (OMA) has earned a reputation as one of the southeast's top arts museums. The fine permanent collection is dominated by pre-Columbian art and American artists such as Georgia O'Keefe, George Inness, and Robert Rauschenberg. These works are supplemented by touring exhibitions from major metropolitan museums, and numerous smaller shows of regional or local significance, although curators tend to avoid overtly controversial works.
See p113.

2 Orlando Science Center

This huge, attention-grabbing, exploratorium-style museum boasts hundreds of interactive, child-friendly exhibits that are designed to introduce kids of all ages to the wonders of science. The center's four floors are divided into 10 themed zones. These deal with subjects ranging from mechanics to math, health and fitness to lasers, making this an educational and fun break from the usual Orlando theme park distractions. Don't miss the CineDome, which houses the planetarium and the world's largest Iwerks® theatre.
See p113.

3 Orange County Regional History Center

Given the region's relatively short history, this museum has wisely ignored geographic limitations. Exhibits not only feature local photographs and memorabilia, but a re-created Victorian parlor, a 1926 fire station, and fascinating temporary shows that cover themes relating to other parts of Florida, such as pirates and space travel. See p113.

4 Charles Hosmer Morse Museum of American Art

Here rests the world's most comprehensive collection of work by American artist Louis Comfort Tiffany, best known for his Art Nouveau stained-glass pieces. The museum's highlight is a spectacular chapel Tiffany made for the 1893 World's Columbian Exposition. There are also interesting collections of 19th- and 20th-century American paintings and jewelry. See p119.

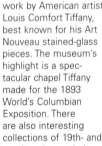

Detail, Charles Hosmer Morse Museum of American Art

5 Cornell Fine Arts Museum

Located on the campus of Rollins College, the small but stylish Cornell is Florida's oldest art collection. It showcases European and American paintings, sculpture, and decorative arts ranging from the Renaissance and Baroque periods to the 20th century. Among the highlights

Historic plane, Flying Tigers Warbird Museum

are *Madonna and Child Enthroned* (c.1480) by Cosimo Rosselli, and *Reclining Figure* by Henry Moore (1982). See p119.

6 Mennello Museum of American Folk Art

This small, lakeside museum houses an unusual and charming collection of paintings by obscure curio-shop owner and Floridian folk artist, Earl Cunningham (1893–1977). In addition to his own work are traveling exhibitions featuring the works of other "outsider" artists. See p113.

7 Flying Tigers Warbird Restoration Museum

If aircraft history is your passion, this is a must-see. Much more than a static museum, the War-bird is a restoration hangar where historic military aircraft are pains-takingly restored to pristine flying condition (those puddles of oil on the floor are real). Visitors can see a P-51 Mustang, a Lockheed P-38 Lightning, a B-17 Flying Fortress, and many others. History and restoration classes are available – as are real flights! See p108.

8 Albin Polasek Museum and Sculpture Gardens

Czech-American Polasek (1879–1965) was a sculptor who specialized in European figurative technique. In semi-retirement, he moved to this self-designed house and studio, where he continued working until his death. The beautiful gardens are filled with his sculptures, as are four galleries within the house, which also hold a few pieces from other artists. See p119.

9 Zora Neale Hurston National Museum of Fine Arts

Eatonville – the first incorporated African-American municipality in the USA – was the childhood home of Zora Neale Hurston (1903–1960), writer, anthropolo-gist, and folklorist. This modest museum offers exhibitions centered on Hurston and the Eatonville of days gone by. See p120.

10 Maitland Historical & Telephone Museums

Artifacts, textiles, and photos from Maitland's pioneer days through to the heydays of the citrus and lumber industries are the focus here. In the same building, the Telephone Museum offers a collection of vintage telephones, and phone memorabilia. ◈ 221 W. Packwood Ave • Map J4 • 407-644-2451 • Open 12-4pm thu–Sun • Free (donation)

Left **Orlando Philharmonic** Right **The Orlando-UCF Shakespeare Festival**

Cultural Venues & Organizations

1 Orlando-UCF Shakespeare Festival

This nationally recognized company has been performing the Bard's works since 1989, and the state-of-the-art John and Rita Lowndes Shakespeare Center has been its home since February 2002. The company is best known for the annual spring festival *(see p64)* at Lake Eola Park, though it mounts high-quality performances throughout the year. ✆ *812 E. Rollins St • Map M4 • 407-893-4600 • Adm*

2 UCF Civic Theatre

Founded as the Orlando Little Theatre in 1926, the Civic has grown into Orlando's version of a Broadway theater. It has three stages and puts on classic and contemporary plays alike. The year-round schedule is packed with high quality shows, but until renovations are complete, most are being staged at the University of Central Florida. ✆ *1001 E. Princeton St • Map M3 • 407-896-7365 • Adm*

3 Theatre Downtown

Recently named Orlando's Best Local Repertory Company, this volunteer organization has been producing first-rate shows since 1984. In 1989, it moved to a former appliance store, and in this casual "Off-Off-Broadway" setting has presented an array of classics, contemporary works (such as David Mamet's *American Buffalo*), and new plays by local writers. ✆ *2113 N. Orange Ave • Map M3 • 407-841-0083 • Adm*

4 Enzian Theater

Central Florida's only full-time art-house cinema is a unique venue – its single-screen, 250-seat house is arranged like a dinner theater, with waiters serving food and drinks (including beer and wine). Featuring foreign and American independents, and with regular special-interest festivals, plus the Florida Film Festival *(see p65)*, this is a place for true cinephiles. *See p121.*

5 SAK Comedy Lab

A downtown favorite, SAK is Orlando's home of improvisation comedy. The SAK players produce shows that are always funny and inventive, and there are two per night. The 8pm shows are usually family-friendly, while the later ones get a bit edgier, although obscene material is strictly avoided. Of particular interest are the series shows, such as *Foolish Hearts*, an ongoing, improvised soap opera. ✆ *380 W. Amelia St • Map P2 • 407-648-0001 • Adm*

Southern Ballet Theater

6 Orlando Philharmonic

Orlando's resident orchestra boasts more than 80 conservatory-trained musicians. Venues vary, and include the Phil's home at Symphony Square, Leu Gardens (for outdoor concerts), and even SeaWorld. Its best-known showcase is the "Phil at Carr", an eight-concert series (Sep–May) at the Bob Carr Performing Arts Center, which features guest artists in both classical and pop concerts. ◈ *Symphony Square, 812 E. Rollins St* • *Map M3* • *407-896-6700* • *Adm*

7 Orlando Opera Company

This respected company has been producing opera since 1979. The season

Orlando Opera Company

(Nov–Apr) is not long – four main shows for three dates each at the Bob Carr Performing Arts Center – but the quality of productions is high, with principle singers brought in from around the country and with music from the Orlando Phil. Smaller shows are also on offer at the Dr. Phillips Center. Ticket prices are very reasonable. ◈ *Dr. Phillips Center for Performing Arts, 1111 N. Orange Ave* • *Map N3* • *407-426-1700* • *Adm*

8 Southern Ballet Theatre

This small, but growing, company presents four major productions annually, including a version of *The Nutcracker*, with the Orlando Philharmonic, choreographed by company artistic director, Fernando Bujones. Smaller shows are held on community stages, but the major productions are at the Bob Carr Performing Arts Centre. ◈ *401 W. Livingston St* • *Map P3* • *407-426-1733* • *Adm*

9 Osceola Center for the Arts

Kissimmee's home of high culture offers a theater, art gallery, and special events. The Osceola Center for the Arts (OCFTA) has an engagingly diverse schedule, eagerly offering a little bit of everything, from Broadway to Barbershop, storytelling to sculptures. ◈ *2411 E. Irlo Bronson Memorial Hwy* • *Map P3* • *407-846-6257* • *Adm*

10 Mad Cow Theatre

A favorite among local actors, this burgeoning theatrical group has developed a reputation for small, high-quality productions. Past plays have ranged from Chekhov to Neil Simon, with a stop at the Orlando International Fringe Festival *(see p65)* for some T.S. Eliot. The productions take place on different stages each year – call the box office for details. ◈ *407-297-8788* • *Adm*

For dinner shows **See pp80–81**

63

Left **Orlando International Fringe Festival** Right **Kissimmee Bluegrass Festival**

🔟 Festivals & Events

1 Renninger's Antique Extravaganzas

From Victorian furnishings to vintage political campaign buttons, you can find all things old and valuable sold at the 1,400 antique stalls spread across a meadow here. The prime goods go fast, so get here early (it opens around 9am). ◈ *Renningers Antique Center, Hwy 441 • Off map • 1-800-522-3555 • 3rd weekend of Jan, Feb, & Nov*

2 Kissimmee Blue-grass Festival

Close harmonies, aching fiddles, and no drums – welcome to the world of bluegrass. Savor the sounds of American folk performers such as The Ramblin' Rose Band and The Osborne Brothers. Lawn chairs are encouraged and camping is available. ◈ *Silver Spurs Arena, 1875 E. Irlo Bronson Hwy • Map H5 • 1-813-783-7205 • 1st weekend of Mar*

Poster, Florida Film Festival

3 Central Florida Fair

This massive 11-day shindig takes place close to Downtown Orlando, but its cowpoke attitude is a world away. The country-style attractions include carnival rides, livestock shows, country music, farming exhibits, and more fried food than you'll ever care to eat. ◈ *4603 W. Colonial Dr • Map C3 • 407-447-1700 • Early Mar*

4 Winter Park Sidewalk Arts Festival

For three days, this prestigious outdoor festival sees hundreds of artists exhibit on sidewalk stalls. Traffic comes to a standstill as massive crowds mill around and ponder purchases. ◈ *Park Ave • Map K4 • 407-672-6390 • Mid-Mar*

5 Orlando-UCF Shakespeare Festival

The highlight of this troupe's nine-month season comes each spring, when they alternate two outdoor productions next to Lake Eola. One is staged traditionally, the other gets a modern twist. ◈ *Walt Disney Amphitheater, Lake Eola Park • Map P3 • 407-447-1700 • Late Mar–Early May*

6 Orlando International Fringe Festival

With more than 500 performances in 10 days, the Fringe offers improvised comedy, drag shows, stand-up, and more. Inspired by the Edinburgh festival, this premier springtime event draws enthusiastic local crowds. ◈ *Various venues • 407-648-0077 • Late Apr or beg May*

7 Zellwood Sweetcorn Festival

The draw here is eating as much sweetcorn as you can while listening to the day-long lineups of excellent country bands. A huge machine, Big Bertha, cooks up to 1,650 ears of corn every nine minutes. There are also some fairground rides and a crafts fair. ◈ 4253 Ponkan Rd • Off map • 407-886-0014 • Mid-May

8 Florida Film Festival
This 10-day festival is packed with more than 100 features, documentaries, and shorts. Film-makers introduce their works, and a few Hollywood names make guest appearances. ◈ Enzian Theater, 1300 S. Orlando Ave, and other venues • Map D4 • 407-629-1088 • Early Jun

9 Gay Days
Gay Days has swelled from a one-day jaunt to a week-long blowout of parties and theme park visits for more than 130,000 gay and lesbian guests. By day, gay and straight mix in the parks; at night, parks and clubs are rented for evening raves. ◈ Various venues • www.gaydays.com • Early Jun

10 Anime Festival Orlando
This gathering of "Japanima-tion" fanatics has screenings, the latest Japanese video games, dance and costume contests, and dozens of dealers offering hard-to-find collectibles. ◈ Hilton Hotel, Altamonte Springs • Map A5 • 3 days in Jun, Jul or Aug

Orlando-UCF Shakespeare Festival

Attraction Events

1 Mardi Gras at Universal
The ultimate 'Big Easy' party, with parades, music, and lots of beaded necklaces. ◈ Universal Studios • Feb–Mar

2 MGM-Studios Star Wars Weekends
Four consecutive weekends of Star Wars-inspired frolics. ◈ Disney-MGM Studios • May

3 Festival Caliente
A sizzling Latin music fiesta with big-name perform-ers and tasty Latin food. ◈ Universal Studios • Late Aug

4 Night of Joy
A two-night showcase of contemporary Christian music. ◈ Disney World • Early Sep

5 Greater Gator Cookoff
Be a judge or compete in this annual alligator-meat cooking competition. ◈ Gatorland • Early Oct

6 Halloween Horror Nights
Universal is transformed into a ghoulish home for the undead. ◈ Universal Studios • Oct–Nov

7 Epcot International Food & Wine Festival
Disney chefs and sommeliers strut their stuff. ◈ Epcot • Oct–Nov

8 ABC Super Soap Weekend
Fans meet and greet soap stars from ABC TV. ◈ Disney-MGM Studios • Early Nov

9 Disney World Festival of the Masters
Daytime art exhibits and night-time big-name jazz shows. ◈ Downtown Disney • Nov

10 Mickey's Very Merry Christmas Party
Evening seasonal fun complete with snow and enchanting pa-rades. ◈ Magic Kingdom • Dec

Left **Donna Karan, Belz Designer Outlet Centre** Right **Nike Factory Store, Belz Factory Outlet World**

Places to Shop

1 Orlando Premium Outlets

Orlando's newest outlet mall is this terrific 110-store complex located just across I-4 from the east entrance of Disney World. It boasts high-end designer outlets by Versace, DKNY, and Barney's New York, as well as an excellent mix of popular brand outlets including Nike, Timberland, and Banana Republic. ◈ *8200 Vineland Ave • Map F3 • 407-238-7787*

2 Belz Factory Outlet World

This branch of Belz is not only the largest and oldest factory outlet mall in Orlando, it's also one of the largest in the U.S.A. Located at the north end of I-Drive, the complex features more than 170 outlets in two fully enclosed malls and four annexes. The best stores focus on mid-line brands such as Nike, The Gap, Oshkosh B'Gosh, Puma, Dockers, Reebok, and Calvin Klein. ◈ *5401 W. Oakridge Rd • Map U1 • 407-354-0126*

3 Belz Designer Outlet Centre

A third of a mile south of Outlet World is this 200,000-sq-ft (18,580-sq-m) strip mall offering nearly 50 decidedly upscale retailers. Fashion-conscious shoppers (both locals and tourists) flock here to cruise the well-stocked outlets of Brooks Brothers, Ann Taylor, Kenneth Cole, Saks Fifth Avenue, Fossil Watches, Donna Karan, Coach, Nine West, Movado, and many others. ◈ *5211 International Dr • Map U1 • 407-352-3632*

4 Florida Mall

Sure, it's a big enclosed suburban mall, but it's also one of the best in Central Florida and hugely popular with visitors and locals. Stores include Burdines, Dillard's, JC Penney, Saks Fifth Avenue, Sears, Nordstrom, Lord & Taylor, and more than 200 others. ◈ *8001 S. Orange Blossom Trail • Map E4 • 407-851-6255*

Park Avenue

5 Park Avenue

This eight-block stretch of downtown Winter Park retains a times-gone-by quality. A canopy of live oak trees shades the brick-paved street, which is surrounded by low buildings and flanked by relaxing Central Park. Many of the stores on this upscale avenue are independents, but there are some national chains too, such as Williams & Sonoma and Banana Republic. There's no food court, but the sidewalks are lined with places for lunch or dinner. ◈ *Park Ave bet Fairbanks Ave & Swoope Ave • Map L4*

Factory outlets – which sell last season's stock and imperfect goods at discounts of at least 30 per cent – generally open 9am–9pm daily.

6 Pointe Orlando

Pointe Orlando is a complex of shopping, dining, and entertainment venues. It offers something for everyone – a 21-screen cinema, the awesome FAO Schwarz toy store (see p101), a Wonder-works entertainment center, seven theme restaurants, plus more than 60 retail stores, including Victoria's Secret, Abercrombie & Fitch, and lots of specialty stores. The landscaped outdoor layout makes this a pleasant place for a shopping spree. ◈ 9101 International Dr • Map T4 • 407-248-2838

Ivanhoe Row

7 Downtown Disney

There are two shopping options in Downtown Disney. On the glittery West Side is the massive Virgin Megastore, George's Guitar Gallery, and more than a dozen one-of-a-kind shops. The more serene Marketplace is highlighted by World of Disney (the planet's largest Disney store) and the LEGO Imagination Center, a massive superstore. ◈ Downtown Disney • Map F2 • 407-824-4321

8 Flea World

Claiming to be America's largest flea market, Sanford's Flea World is a Byzantine maze of more than 1,700 sales booths, which are bursting with bargains every weekend. The mostly new goods are already cheap, but you can haggle to lower prices still. In addition to an A to Z list of goods for sale, Flea World also has live bands, bingo, and an a old-style amusement park, Fun World, for the kids. ◈ 4311 S. Hwy 17/92, Sanford • Off map • 407-330-1792 • Open 9am–6pm Fri–Sun

9 Renninger's Antique & Flea Markets

Spread across a bucolic country meadow, Renninger's offers a large, folksy flea market, and a diverse indoor and outdoor antique market. The flea market offers everything from clothing to vinyl. The antique market has permanent dealers who specialize in excellent furnishings and jewelry. Renninger's also hosts the massive Antique Extravaganzas (see p64). ◈ 20651 Hwy 441, 1 m (1.6 km) E. of Mount Dora • Off map • 1-352-383-8393

10 Ivanhoe Row

This stretch of antique shops has thinned in recent years due to rising rents, but there are still more than a dozen stores offering vintage linens, clothing, jewelry, and various collectables. The period furniture available can range from Art Deco to Victorian. ◈ North Orange Ave • Map N3

Factory outlet stores often have sales at the same times of the year as regular shops (Mar–Apr and Aug–Oct).

Left **The Boheme** Right **Ran-Getsu of Tokyo**

10 High-End Restaurants

1 Victoria & Albert's
The high price can limit this to very special occasions, but trust the first-class food, fine wine, and faultless staff to make a memorable visit. It's decorated like Queen Victoria's dining room, and each table gets its very own Victoria and Albert as servers. Changing menus offer seven courses of international dishes, including apple-smoked Colorado bison and black bass with couscous. Take advantage of the wine-pairings (a glass with each of the five courses); it's cheaper and more varied than buying a bottle. See p94.

2 Manuel's on the 28th
The panorama from the floor-to-ceiling windows in this often lively 28th-floor eatery is unbeatable. The menu changes each season and might feature phyllo-wrapped lamb loin with spinach-boursin stuffing, yellowfin tuna in a green curry-and-ginger crust,

Emeril's of Orlando

and Chilean sea bass with lump crab. Manuel's has one of the best wine lists in town. See p117.

3 California Grill
The 15th-floor vista here gets top marks from both critics and diners (especially when the lights are dimmed for Magic Kingdom's nightly fireworks display), as does the Pacific Rim cuisine. Popular choices are seared grouper in a noodle bowl with ginger-crab salad, and pork tenderloin with polenta and mushrooms. There are also interesting vegetarian and sushi menus. It's hard to get a table on weekends. See p94.

4 Emeril's of Orlando
Famous US TV chef Emeril Lagasse owns this place, but only appears once a month, leaving the day-to-day cooking of the creole-inspired menu to his chefs. They create treats such as quail stuffed with Louisiana oyster dressing, andouille-crusted redfish, and a kosher salt and cracked black pepper rib-eye steak. This lofty place has a 12,000-bottle wine cellar. It's tough to get a table for dinner unless you book early, but there's a similar lunch menu at two-thirds of the price. ◎ CityWalk • Map T1 • 407-224-2424 • $$$$$

5 La Coquina
An imaginative beef, poultry, and seafood menu makes La Coquina the most acclaimed of the Hyatt Regency's five eateries. The veal tenderloin with sake-

For price ranges **See p95**

Maison & Jardin

glazed prawns, and the sugar
cane-skewered scallops with rice
grits and artichokes are two hits.
Try the famous Sunday brunch,
with its unlimited champagne and
huge array of hot and cold dishes.
❧ 1 Grand Cypress Blvd • Map F2 • 407-
239-1234 • Smoke-free • No kids' menu
• Pre-arrange vegetarian entrees • $$$$

6 Ran-Getsu of Tokyo
Sushi and sashimi are the big
draw here. Try *tekka-don* (tender
slices of tuna) or *una-ju* (grilled eel
fillets), favorites of more adventurous diners. *Yosenabe,* a soup
that blends seafood, chicken, and
duck, is another popular choice.
A Japanese drum group performs
twice a night (Thu–Sat) and koi
ponds and Japanese gardens
outside help keep the mood
peaceful. *See p105.*

7 The Boheme
Seafood and game are the
stars at this stylish downtown
restaurant. Fans of pan-seared fish
can try the Chilean sea
bass or the Dover sole.
Atlantic salmon is
painted with an apricot-
horseradish glaze and
grilled. Gamier tastes
are met with pheasant
breast and sausage
with pistachio-roast
garlic stuffing, and
grilled venison sirloin
with boar sausage.
There's a kids' menu as
well. *See p117.*

8 Maison & Jardin
Swiss chef Hans Spirig has
spent 17 years honing the menu
at this elegant restaurant. Well-
heeled diners tuck into pan-seared
quail and ostrich tenderloin with
wild mushrooms, and veal with
Maine lobster and morels. In addition to à la carte, there are two
fixed-price menus and a 1,200-
variety wine list. Advance reservations are essential. They'll make
chicken Alfredo for kids. *See p123.*

9 Park Plaza Gardens
For a touch of class, book a
table at the exquisite Park Plaza
Gardens. The glorious cuisine
(such as blackened deep sea
grouper with red lentils and curry
vinaigrette) is enjoyed in a divine
garden, much like a French courtyard. Take your pick from one of
the best wine lists in Orlando, and
finish off with towering desserts
such as key lime pie. *See p123.*

10 Siam Orchid
A crowd of well-heeled
regulars and newcomers mix in
the intimate rooms and split-level
dining room of this upscale Thai
eatery. Perennial favorites include
pad thai (rice noodles with ground
pork, seafood, crushed peanuts,
and a sweet sauce) and *royal thai,*
with chicken, potatoes, and onions
in a yellow curry sauce. *See p105.*

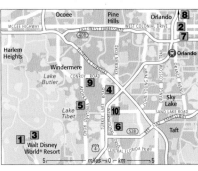

*Unless stated, all restaurants advise reservations, take credit cards,
and have DA, smoking tables, kids' menus, A/C, and vegetarian dishes.*

69

Left **Outback Steakhouse** Right **Café Tu Tu Tango**

🔟 Family Restaurants

1 Rainforest Café
This jungle-themed restaurant provides noisy fun and a California-style menu. The mixed grill includes barbecued ribs, soy-ginger steak skewers, chicken breast, and peppered shrimp. Kids get their own special menu, the cartoon-like decor is good fun, and a "volcano" erupts every now and then. *See p95.*

Bergamo's

2 Romano's Macaroni Grill
Despite being part of a chain, Romano's has a neighborhood feel. The modestly priced Italian menu includes thin-crust pizzas cooked in a wood-burning oven, sauteed salmon scaloppini, and chicken marsala. Paper tablecloths and crayons will keep kids happy for hours. ✎ *12148 Apopka-Vineland Rd • Map F2 • 407-239-6676 • $*

3 Coral Reef Restaurant
A 600,000-gallon (272,600-liter) floor-to-ceiling aquarium is a calming backdrop to this themed restaurant. Despite the high-brow, mainly fish and seafood menu, it's very child-friendly. Try the sauteed rock shrimp in a lemon cream sauce. *See p95.*

4 Outback Steakhouse
Tasty seared steaks are the headliners here; choose from rib-eyes, strips, fillets, and porterhouses. The Outback also serves good smoked ribs, shrimp and chicken over fettucine, rib-and-chicken combos, pork chops, and hamburgers. ✎ *4845 S. Kirkman Rd • Map D3 • 407-292-5111 • $$$*

5 Restaurant Marrakesh
Mosaic tiles and a painted Moorish ceiling set the Moroccan scene. The food is flavorsome, with delights such as roast lamb *au jus* with couscous, and marinated beef shish kabobs. A belly dancer shimmies around and kids love to join her. *See p95.*

6 Café Tu Tu Tango
The menu in this lofty space is Spanish tapas in name but more international in flavor, with such diverse nibbles as baked goat's cheese, tuna sashimi, alligator bites, and snapper fingers. Performers (from sword eaters to artists at work) provide the entertainment. *See p105.*

7 Bergamo's
At this restaurant, the waiters sing Broadway tunes and opera while the chefs prepare the Italian menu. It covers all bases, with pasta, meat, and seafood – try the lobster, shrimp, clams, and mussels in a white wine and garlic sauce, or the veal T-bone

Unless stated, all restaurants advise reservations, take credit cards, and have DA, smoking tables, kids' menus, A/C, and vegetarian dishes.

with olive and anchovy butter.
⊛ The Mercado, 8445 International Dr
• Map T3 • 407-352-3805 • $$$

Baja Burrito Kitchen
8 The draw here is the fresh and healthy Californian and Mexican cusine, with tacos, quesadillas, fajitas, and burritos, stuffed with lean meat and sour cream and cheese. ⊛ 2716 E. Colonial Dr • Map N4 • 407-895-6112 • Smoke-free • $

Panera Bread
9 There are no preservatives in the dough used in the sandwiches and baked goods available to eat in or take away; there's everything from wholegrain to focaccia and sourdough. Soup is also available. ⊛ 7828 Sand Lake Rd • Map F3 • 407-226-6992 • Smoke-free • $

Chili's Grill & Bar
10 This international Tex-Mex chain serves scrumptious Cajun chicken sandwiches, margarita-grilled chicken topped with lime shrimp, and Cadillac fajitas with black beans and rice. See p105.

Chili's Grill & Bar

Dining with Disney & Universal Characters

1 Chef Mickey's
Mickey hosts American buffet breakfasts and dinners in the Contemporary Resort.

2 Restaurantosaurus
Donald Duck and pals host the Breakfastosaurus in the Animal Kingdom every morning.

3 Wonderland Tea Party
Every weekday at 1:30pm, Alice in Wonderland characters join guests in the Grand Floridian resort for tea and cakes.

4 1900 Park Fare
Have breakfast with Mary Poppins or a sit-down dinner with other Disney favorites at the Grand Floridian Resort.

5 Mickey's Backyard BBQ
Disney characters keep you entertained at this hoedown and all-you-can-eat American buffet dinner in Fort Wilderness.

6 Cinderella's Royal Table
A whole host of Disney characters join you for the "Once Upon a Time" breakfast in Magic Kingdom's Cinderella castle (park adm required).

7 Circus McGurkus
The Cat in the Hat, the Grinch, Thing One, and Thing Two turn up at Seuss Landing in Islands of Adventure at 2:45pm daily for a late lunch.

8 The Crystal Palace
Meet Pooh and his cohorts for American buffet breakfasts, lunches, and dinners in Magic Kingdom (park adm required).

9 Liberty Tree Tavern
Mickey and Goofy host the sit-down dinner "Liberate your Appetite" in the Magic Kingdom (park adm required).

10 Cape May Café
Join Goofy for a breakfast buffet at the Beach Club Resort.

For character meals, call seven days in advance (Disney: 407-939-3463; Universal: 407-363-8000). Expect to pay $ for kids, $$–$$$ for adults.

Left **Bar, Bar-B-Q Bar** Right **Downtown bar scene**

Places to Have a Drink

1 Metropolis

In a stylish velvet and cherry-wood venue, Metropolis achieves an upscale ambience often aspired to but rarely achieved in Orlando's clubs. DJs and a dance floor cater to groups of friends out for a giggle, while dark corners offer privacy for couples who want to smooch and sip cocktails. Top-class facilities include billiards tables and plenty of comfortable seating to encourage lounging around. *See p104.*

2 Knock Knock

This venue looks a bit like a submarine in *20,000 Leagues Under The Sea*, with its porthole windows and distressed metal. An eclectic crowd – from models to business moguls – hang out around the circular bar listening to ambient tunes. *See p116.*

3 8 Seconds

Country music and line-dancing are the main draws here, but this massive former factory, with its dozen bars, also has a pool room upstairs, bull-riding out back, and a live band in the barn outside. This is a good place to check out the pulse of Orlando's urban cowboy population. *See p116.*

4 The Bar at California Grill

This bar is a fabulous place to kick back, enjoy a bottle of wine and watch the fireworks over the Magic Kingdom. The secret is out, though, so come early for a table. Finding a spot at other times isn't too hard as long as you avoid the dinner rush. *See p94.*

5 Fiddler's Green

A big, noisy Irish pub, Fiddler's Green has an excellent beer selection, a homey, shabby ambience, and a bartender who pours faster than anyone in town. Darts and occasional live music form the entertainment, but people come here just to down a few beers and shoot the breeze. Lunch and dinner are served. *See p122.*

Bar-B-Q Bar

  Most bars tend to open betweem 4–8pm and close around 2am.

6 Bar-B-Q Bar

It's little more than an average beer joint with sticky floors and loud crowds, but Bar-B-Q is *the* place to see and be seen for the more creative set. A favorite venue with local musicians, the bar gets packed whenever there's a good band on stage. People-watch clubbers cruising the Orange Avenue strip from a sidewalk table. ✆ *64 N. Orange Ave • Map P3*

7 Sky 60

Located above The Social *(see p74)*, this rooftop bar is an Orange Avenue hotspot, attracting

Fiddler's Green

folks who prefer not to mingle with the masses but rather look down on them. Covered in whitewash, this airy spot is a classier option for folks who usually drink downstairs or at the Bar-B-Q Bar. Entertainment is typically provided via a DJ who leans toward to refined, less aggressive grooves. ✆ *60 N. Orange Ave • Map P3*

8 The Bösendorfer Lounge

Luxury is a tough sell Downtown, in partly because the club crowd tends to be well under 30 and lacking serious funds. However, this swanky hotel bar is thriving, confirming that an older, upscale, and urbane crowd is more than willing to pay the price for a suave evening of fancy cocktails. *See p116.*

9 Dexter's of Thornton Park

A white-collar after-work crowd frequents this hugely popular bar/

restaurant in a spacious, loft-like room. On fine nights, drinkers often head for the small outdoor space or spill out onto the sidewalk, jostling and juxtaposing with the folk from the fundamentalist church and a working-class beer joint that are located on the same street. Dexter's is also known for its great New American menu, and for serving dozens of wines by the glass. There's another branch in Winter Park *(see p122)*. ✆ *808 E. Washington St • Map P3*

10 AKA Lounge

With more name changes than there are new moons, and an entrance that's tough to find (look for a doorway adjacent to the Pine Street Grill), it's a bit of a challenge to find your way into this bar. But the effort is well worth it, as this is one of Downtown's most comfortable and appealing drinking spots. The lounge occupies the top floors of two merged brownstones, offering plenty of space, a full bar, plenty of contemporary artwork, and a fine line-up of DJs and live bands. ✆ *68 E. Pine St • Map P3 • No DA*

The minimum age requirement for drinkers in Florida is 21 years. Be sure to bring photo ID to avoid being turned away at the door.

73

Left **Hard Rock Live** right **Beer bottles, Will's Pub**

Live Music Venues

1 The Social

The Social (formerly known as Sapphire) serves up an eclectic mix of live music. Sounds range from alternative rock to funk, jazz, and dance, with local DJs also gracing the club's legendary stage. For years, the club's policy of booking top national touring acts meant it was the shining light of Orlando's live music scene. Competition from much larger clubs is stiffer now, but this tiny spot, with its stylishly raw decor, remains O-Town's favorite spot to enjoy live music. *See p116.*

2 House of Blues

Wall-to-wall original folk art gives this giant venue a funky look. But like all things in the Disney empire, the decor hides a modern, smooth-running machine. HOB books amazing acts in every genré, from hip-hop to death-metal. Unlike many clubs, shows start and end on time, and the sound system is crystal clear. The one flaw is an incredible lack of seating with stage views, so be prepared to be on your feet all night. *See p93.*

3 Hard Rock Live

The ying to HOB's yang, Hard Rock has a more comfortable room, with balcony seating and good stage views. The grand ballroom decor is more apropos for acts that want to perform in an elegant setting, so it's not surprising that top R&B artists such as Maxwell and Erykah Badu play here. The Hard Rock schedule is more erratic, with fewer top name bookings. *See p104.*

4 Will's Pub

This tiny dive has earned a reputation among local musicians for being one of the best-loved music clubs in town, with a line-up of punk, ska, and alternative rock bands. The back room stage is small and the ceiling low, but the PA is loud and the beer list huge. The front room has a pool table, and there's a patio out front in case fresh air is required. ◉ *1850 N. Mills Ave • Map M3 • 407-898-5070*

5 The Bösendorfer Lounge

The lounge music craze that swept the nation a few years ago has almost vanished, leaving only serious practitioners. This elegant hotel bar is a swell place to sip cocktails and dig the duet in evening dress who sing near the $250,000 Bösendorfer Grand piano. Maybe it's the heavy drapes, the dark wood, or the well-tuned ennui of some patrons, but you feel wealthy just being here. *See p116.*

6 Blues Bar at House of Blues

Before it evolved into a chain of mega-clubs, the original HOB concept was closer to this casual roadhouse place, which offers bayou-inspired eats, cold beer, and live blues bands on a low

Almost everyone needs to show ID to get into Orlando's clubs, most of which are for over 21's only; others set higher age limits.

stage. Though they get little promotion, the bands booked here are excellent. And even if dinner prices are inflated (à la everything at Disney), the cover charge is zero. See p116.

7 Adobe Gilas
The downside to Gilas is that they book mostly cover bands. The upside is a young, good-looking crowd getting smashed on tequila and dirty dancing with near strangers. The band usually sets up on the patio, but it's more fun and sweaty when it rains and the band crams itself into an inside corner. Sure, the southwestern theme decor gets old fast, but if you need to relive the days of dorm parties, this is the place to go. See p104.

8 Bodhisattva Social Club
In Downtown's always-changing scene, this small club has evolved into one of the hippest. Upstairs in the two-story brownstone is where it happens – an assortment of oddball performers do their thing in a space that looks like an abandoned living room. The schedule ranges from free-form open mic to acoustic acts, from DJs to original bebop big bands. See p116.

9 Fairbanks Inn (aka FBI)
Old rockers don't die; they just lose their record deals and start playing here. Orlando's home to hard rock and metal is a strange venue offering pool tables, video games, and a PA that can make your ears bleed. The schedule is heavy with local headbangers, and national acts

Fairbanks Inn

occasionally appear. ◎ 1788 W. Fairbanks Ave • Map L3 • 407-647-0704

10 Peter Scott's
Upscale, refined, elegant; these words are rarely used to describe Orlando music venues, but they're fitting for Peter Scott's. It boasts an excellent (if expensive) restaurant, a lush leather and marble decor, and mellow sounds of live jazz and swing. Sometimes they book a national act from way back (like Leslie Gore). Otherwise, catch Orlando's own rising stars Michael Andrew and Swingerhead when they're on. ◎ 1811 W. State Rd 434, Longwood • Map P3 • 407-834-4477

Left **Tabu** Right **Downtown nightlife scene**

TOP 10 Hip Clubs

1 Matrix
This 15,000-sq ft (1,480 sq m) venue takes the prize for Orlando's coolest new dance club. Copping style points from the film after which it's named, Matrix offers an upscale industrial decor with a cobalt blue and stainless steel color scheme, a gigantic computerized lighting rig above the dance floor, and walls of video screens. Orlando house, techno, and electronica rule the decks. *See p104.*

Blue Room

2 Tabu
Co-owned by one of the Backstreet Boys, this former theater is now a darkly stylish and cavernous club. The main floor boasts two large bars, a big dance floor, and video screens. Occasionally, the old upstairs balcony is transformed into a late-night sushi bar, and the lobby sometimes has a roster of supporting DJs. Lines can be long, especially when there's a big-name DJ or PA on. *See p116.*

3 The Club
Once named top club in the US by *Rolling Stone* magazine, The Club occupies the sprawling interior of one of Orlando's oldest buildings. The magic ingredients (vast size, an awe-inspiring light and sound system, and an international DJ lineup) still make this the best night out in Orlando. The Club attracts a mixed crowd that is very gay-friendly. The sounds runs from trance to hip-hop to Latin, depending on the night of the week. ◎ *578 N. Orange Ave • Map N3 • 407-872-0066 • Occasional adm*

4 Cairo
Who could have guessed ancient Egypt would make such a splendid theme for a dance club? In between the Sphinx paintings and columns in this multi-level space, clubbers dance to alternative house, disco, retro-progressive music, and more. Upstairs, an excellent rooftop lounge known as the Reggae Bar features reggae and other downtempo beats. When there's a line stretching down the block, duck into Knock Knock *(see p116)* next door and have a drink. *See p116.*

5 Icon
Between the futuristic metal decor, the barely dressed cage dancers, and the steady beat of house music, Icon is a trendy slice of Downtown's club scene. Tucked into the first floors of an otherwise nondescript office building, Icon's main room is a

surprisingly big, multi-level affair, with a hefty sound system that can rattle teeth. As with most Downtown clubs, things get moving fairly late on. *See p116.*

6 Empire

This lakeside venue goes for overkill with laser and pyrotechnic shows. DJs spin trance, techno, and house, with some nights designated all-gay, others mixed. When the dance floor heats up, the lakeside terrace offers welcome relief and an occasional breeze. ⚘ *4315 N. Orange Blossom Trail • Map L1 • 407-522-0411 • Adm*

Empire

7 Blue Room

With a single-story interior, this downtown club is more intimate than some local options. The Blue Room excels with a comfortably upscale vibe, making it less of a meat-market than other clubs in this area. There's lots of room around the bar to chat, if you can be heard over the progressive house beats. Top DJs have residencies here. ⚘ *17 W. Pine St • Map P3 • 407-423-2588 • Closed Mon & Wed*

8 Mannequins

Pleasure Island's 21-and-over dance club is the real deal, not some Mickey Mouse knock-off of a modern club. The decor is surprisingly dark and foreboding, with an eerie industrial interior that wouldn't look out of place in a dominatrix den. The dance floor revolves while the DJs

spin techno and house. If hip, young celebrities are visiting Disney, they'll likely end up here at some point. *See p93.*

9 Caribbean Beach Club

While most of O-Town grooves to house, techno and electronica, the sizeable Caribbean Beach Club jams to the earthier vibes. Expect Latin, disco, calypso, soca, and reggae sounds, which pack in an ethnically diverse crowd. ⚘ *4919 W. Colonial Dr • Map C3 • 407-299-0706*

10 Roxy

Tucked into an after-dark desert area of town, the Roxy is a big multi-floor dance club, with impressive hip-hop, Latin, and house DJs playing nightly. The loyal following tends to be less self-consciously trendy and more hetero than the usual downtown club mix. Monday Night Fights see amateur boxers from the crowd knock back a few beers then jump in a ring to fight each other. Well, the crowd *is* different to that found in Downtown. ⚘ *740 Bennett Rd • Map N5 • 407-898-4004*

For more information on nightlife **See pp72–5**

Left **Moodswing Café** Right **Carmello, the Orlando drag queen diva**

Gay & Lesbian Hangouts

1 Parliament House Resort

Parliament is one of the southeast's premier gay resorts, boasting non-stop entertainment. Beside a 130-room hotel, there's a pulsating dance club, a piano bar, a country and western bar, a video bar, lakeside beach parties, and more. ✆ *410 N. Orange Blossom Trail • Map P2 • 407-425-7571 • Free (Adm to club)*

2 Southern Nights

Regularly named Orlando's best gay nightclub, this is a sizeable party hotspot on the weekends (Friday and Sunday for him, Saturday for her). Techno and house rule, except on Mondays, when it's Latin night. Drag shows and special events are always on the calendar. ✆ *375 S. Bumby Ave • Map P4 • 407-898-0424 • Adm*

3 Empire

This massive lakeside venue features a killer sound system and a great light show. On Friday, the club attracts mixed crowds with DJs spinning trance music, while Saturday is mostly gay with techno and house. On Sunday afternoons there's a beach party and buffet, adding a little sun and fun to the DJ's mix. *See p77.*

4 Full Moon Saloon

If your favorite Village Person was the Cowboy, the Full Moon is for you. It's a country and western club where hundreds of butch dudes in chaps and hats two-step their cares away. There's also a large contingent of manly leather types. The club is big, the outside space is huge, and it's considered a Sunday afternoon hot spot. ✆ *500 N. Orange Blossom Trail • Map N2 • 407-648-8725 • Free*

5 The Peacock Room

The Peacock's jazzy ambience is a welcome respite from the thump of techno. This is a small, stylish lounge in the heart of

Empire

Orlando's Top 10

Orlando's gay-friendly ViMi district. The decor is muted Art Deco and a small jazz band often plays. The cool vibe also attracts straights, making for a nice mix. ⚲ *1321 N. Mills Ave • Map N4 • 407-228-0048 • Free*

6 Cactus Club

Cactus is Orlando's anti-trend gay club. There are no strippers or drag queens racing around here. Instead, expect a low-key, friendly neighborhood bar with darts, pool, and a nice outdoor patio. ⚲ *1300 N. Mills Ave • Map N4 • 407-894-3041 • Free*

Southern Nights

7 The Club

Ensconced within a former Firestone garage, this giant venue has long been rated one of the southeast's top dance clubs, particularly with gays, ravers, and all types trendy. Although gay-only nights are gone, the Club continues to pump out house, hip-hop, and trance music for "the community." The upstairs Glass Chamber is a relaxing chill-out room with comfy couches. *See p76.*

8 Club Orlando

If you like to get sweaty by working out rather than dancing, Club Orlando (part of a chain of health resorts for gay men) is the spot to head for. Open 24 hours, this upscale facility has state-of-the-art equipment, a heated outdoor pool, a ten-man sunken hot tub, Jacuzzi, steam room, tropical garden, and regular parties. One-day memberships are available for visitors. ⚲ *450 E. Compton St • Map P3 • 407-425-5005 • Adm*

9 Faces

A long-time favorite for local lesbians, this homey place is busiest on weekends, when DJs up the tempo with house music. The bar staff's friendly vibe, plus pool, darts, and pinball, are other selling points. The first Saturday of each month is Latin night. ⚲ *4910 Edgewater Dr • Map L1 • 407-291-7571 • Free*

10 Moodswing Café

"Be yourself" is the slogan of this stylish little eatery. The room has different colored areas, each representing a mood (if you're hungry, go sit in "greed"). Although it doesn't bill itself as a gay establishment, the Sunday Drag Brunch is a bit of a give-away, as the wait staff and some customers dress to impress. ⚲ *815 N. Mills Ave • Map N3 • 407-895-9777 • Free*

For more on Orlando's clubs See pp76–7

Left **Medieval Times** Right **Sleuth's Mystery Dinner Theatre**

Dinner Shows

1 Hoop-Dee-Doo Musical Revue

Book early for Disney's most popular "chow-and-cheer" night. The jokes are silly, the stars dress in costumes from Broadway's *Oklahoma!*, and if you don't join in the sing-along fun, the actors and audience will keep on at you until you do. Dinner is all-you-can-eat fried-chicken and barbecue ribs; a vegetarian menu is available with 24 hours' notice. *Disney's Fort Wilderness Resort • Map F2 • 407-939-3463 • 5, 7:15, & 9:30pm nightly*

2 Arabian Nights

Horses steal this show. Several breeds such as chiseled Arabians and muscular Belgians thunder through a performance including Wild West trick riding, chariot races, a little slapstick comedy, and bareback daredevilry. Horse fans can pet the four-legged stars after the show. *6225 W. Irlo Bronson Memorial Hwy • Map G2 • 407-239-9223 • 7:30pm nightly*

3 Medieval Times

Horses take a secondary role at this spectacle. Instead, the action heroes are knights who get into sword fights, joust, and otherwise raise the roof while you feast on the likes of barbecued ribs, and roasted chicken with your fingers (after all, this is the 11th century). If you arrive early, you can tour a re-created medieval village. *4510 W. Irlo Bronson Memorial Hwy • Map G3 • 407-396-1518 • Show times vary*

4 Polynesian Luau Dinner Show

High-energy performers from Hawaii, New Zealand, and Tahiti show off their hula, ceremonial, and fire-dancing in an open-air theater. Meanwhile, tuck into the all-you-can-eat meal, which includes roast pork and chicken, fried rice, vegetables, and fruit. Learn how to make *leis* and do the hula in the pre-show. *Disney's Polynesian Resort • Map F1 • 407-939-3463 • 5:15 & 8pm nightly*

5 Pirates Dinner Adventure

The swashbuckling actors entertain with comedy, drama, and music, on a set that is is a full-size pirate ship on a water-filled "lagoon". The dinner buffet features roast chicken, braised beef, herbed rice, and more. After the show, there's a Buccaneer Bash

Arabian Nights

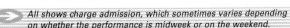

All shows charge admission, which sometimes varies depending on whether the performance is midweek or on the weekend.

Dance Party to help you burn a few of those spare calories. ❧ 6400 Carrier Dr • Map U2 • 407-248-0590 • 7:45pm nightly

6 Aloha! Polynesian Luau Dinner & Show

The Hawaiian Rhythms dance troupe delivers a song-and-fire-dance show. The luau is one of the better meals on the Orlando dinner-show circuit. The menu

Pirates Dinner Adventure

includes mahi mahi (dolphin fish) in pina colada sauce, sweet-and-sour chicken, smoked pork, vegetables, rice, dessert, and beverages including one cocktail. The show is inside the park, but theme-park admission is not required. ❧ SeaWorld • Map T2 • 407-363-2559 • 6:30pm nightly

7 Sleuth's Mystery Dinner Theatre

The theater's cast stages eight different shows over the course of a month, all with a suspicious death and a twist before the mystery is uncovered. Meals include hors d'oeuvres before the show, then your choice of honey-glazed Cornish game hen, prime rib, or lasagna with side dishes, dessert, and unlimited beer, wine, and sodas. ❧ 7508 Universal Blvd • Map T1 • 407-363-1985 • Show times vary

8 Capone's Dinner & Show

Settle into the 1930s and visit Al Capone's notorious speakeasy, a place where pseudo-mobsters and their molls entertain guests with a lot of song and dance. The all-you-can-eat buffet offers pasta, sausage with peppers and onions, baked chicken and ham, vegetables, potatoes, and whatever beer, wine, coffee, iced tea and sodas you care to drink.

❧ 4740 W. Irlo Bronson Memorial Hwy • Map G3 • 407-397-2378 • 8pm nightly

9 MurderWatch Mystery Theatre

In a twist on the normal murder mystery, the cast here acts out four possible endings to the story; the audience has to figure out which one is the correct plot. The crimes take place in a 19th-century-style restaurant, while guests partake of a buffet of prime rib, pasta, and more. ❧ 1850 Hotel Plaza Blvd • Map G2 • 407-850-9555 • 6 & 9pm Sat

10 Mark Two Dinner Theater

Broadway fans will love this place, which performs musicals by Rodgers & Hammerstein, George M. Cohan, and other American theater legends. It's no rival to the London or New York stages, but it's a good show. A varied menu feeds the parts the songs can't reach. ❧ 3376 Edgewater Dr • Map M2 • 407-843-6275 • 8pm Wed–Sat

There is no minimum age limit for dinner shows, although some may be unsuitable for younger children.

Left **Clearwater Beach, Gulf Coast** Right **Florida Aquarium**

🔟 Day Trips West

1 Busch Gardens

With five roller coasters, this park is a close second to Islands of Adventure (see pp20–23) on the thrill front. Roller coaster addicts rate the park's Kumba ride very highly. Busch Gardens is also a step ahead of Disney's Animal Kingdom (see pp18–19) when it comes to spotting nature's finest creatures, which are very visible here on the Serengeti Plain, Serengeti Safari Tour, and Rhino Rally ride. During summer don't miss cool rides like Congo River Rapids and Tanganyika Tidal Wave. ✆ 3000 E. Busch Blvd, Tampa • Open 9:30am–6pm daily • Adm

Busch Gardens

2 Florida Aquarium

Florida's native species are just a fraction of the more than 10,000 animals and plants on display in this modern attraction. Wetlands, bays, coral reefs, and their creatures are featured in several galleries, and you can watch divers feed sharks and

other marine creatures. ✆ 701 Channelside Dr, Tampa • Open 9:30am–5pm daily • Adm

3 Lowry Park Zoo

Tampa's first zoo has 1,500 creatures, including Sumatran tigers, Persian leopards, and Komodo dragons. It also serves as a rehabilitation center for injured manatees (see p31) and as a sanctuary for Florida panthers and red wolves. A free-flight aviary and petting zoo provide a chance to touch some tamer species. ✆ 7530 N. Blvd, Tampa • Open 9:30am–5pm daily • Adm

4 Ybor City/Centro Ybor

The Latin heart of Tampa contains the Ybor State Museum, plus trendy art galleries and lively cafés that are thronged by day. Take the opportunity to try a Cuban sandwich and strong café cubano, or at night, to salsa and merengue into the small hours in one of the district's dozen or so clubs. ✆ Seventh Ave, Tampa • Off Map

5 Florida International Museum

The museum's Kennedy Collection includes the rocking chair JFK used to soothe his ailing back, as well as full-scale re-creations of the White House's Oval Office and Rose Garden. The other main draws are the traveling exhibitions from major international collections. ✆ 100 2nd St N., St Petersburg • Open 9am–6pm Mon–Sat, noon–6pm Sun • Adm

6 The Gulf Beaches

Western Pinellas County has more than 30 miles (48 km) of white-sand, low-surf, warm-water beaches that are highly popular throughout the year. St. Pete Beach, Treasure Island, Madeira Beach, and Clearwater Beach are among the many headliners. *St. Pete Beach to Clearwater Beach • Off Map*

7 Deep Sea Fishing & Sightseeing

Land a whopper on fishing trips into the Gulf of Mexico. Commonly caught species include grouper, amberjack, and red snapper. Alternatively, there are sightseeing excursions that offer encounters with dolphins, sea birds, and, on occasion, manatees. *Hubbard's Marina • 150 St. John's Pass Boardwalk, Madeira Beach • 1-727-393-1947 • Adm • No DA*

8 Swim with the Manatees

Few natural thrills compare to snorkeling or scuba diving with these gentle, endangered giants, sometimes called sea cows. The manatees frequent the springs and rivers of West Citrus County (about two hours drive north of St. Petersburg) much of the year, but even more so from November through March. Several outfits offer various two-hour trips. *US Hwy 19, Crystal River • 1-352-795-3149 • Adm • No DA*

9 Caladesi Island State Park

This 3-mile (5-km) island, accessible by ferry from Honeymoon Island, is a lovely outdoor retreat traversed by a nature trail. A ban on cars

Annie Pfeiffer Chapel, Florida Southern College

helps keep it much as it was a century ago. In season, beach areas are dotted with the tracks of loggerhead turtles that nest here. *Ferry to island • 3 Causeway Blvd, Dunedin • Ferry runs 10am–5pm daily • Adm • Off Map*

10 Florida Southern College

In the late 1930s, renowned architect Frank Lloyd Wright designed 12 campus buildings at this college – the world's largest collection. Highlights include the Annie Pfeiffer Chapel, the Roux Library, the Danforth Chapel, and the Esplanades. Pick up a walking-tour map from the visitor center. *111 Lake Hollingsworth Dr, Lakeland • Visitors center open 11am–4pm Tue–Fri, 10am–2pm Sat, 2–4pm Sun • Free*

For Day Trips North & East See pp84–5

Left **Daytona Beach** Right **Ron Jon Surf Shop, Cocoa Beach**

TOP 10 Day Trips North & East

1 Kennedy Space Center
This well-conceived monument to America's space program impresses visitors with exhibits both mammoth, such as the Saturn V Rocket, and minuscule, such as antiquated space suits. Bus tours are a good way to take in the installations. *See pp38–41.*

2 Cocoa Beach
Just 60 miles (96 km) west of I-4 via the Bee Line Expressway, Cocoa Beach is the seashore closest to Orlando. The beach is picturesque, although the surrounding town is less so (apart from the lovely Cocoa Village near US Hwy 1). Surfing is taken seriously here, due in part to the presence of the Ron Jon Surf Shop, a vast surfing mecca that sells surf wear, beach gear, boards, and every imaginable beach accessory. ⊗ *Off map*

3 Daytona Beach
During the annual "Spring Break," this legendary beach (just 90 minutes from Orlando along I-4) is the destination for thousands of vacationing college students, who drink and party until they drop. But sun and fun isn't all that's offered. Beach Street is lined with shops, restaurants, and clubs; Klassix Auto Attraction features 120 cars, both vintage and one-offs; and of course, there's the Daytona Speedway, home to the Daytona 500 and other NASCAR races *(see p57).*
⊗ *Off map • Tourist info 1-904-255-0415*

4 New Smyrna Beach
Just south of Daytona Beach, New Smyrna is a smaller, calmer town that lacks Daytona's party scene. The white sand beach is picture perfect – but as at Daytona, cars share the space with sunworshipers. For food, the place to go is JB's Fish Camp, a raucous and friendly shack beside Mosquito Lagoon, which serves some of the state's tastiest fish, seafood, and key lime pie. ⊗ *Off map*

Swimming at Katie's Wekiva River Landing

5 Southern Cassadaga Spiritualist Camp
Buried deep in the woods near exit 54 off I-4, tiny Cassadaga was founded more than 100 years ago as a community of clairvoyants, mediums, and healers. Resident spiritualists promote the science, philosophy, and religion of Spiritualism; offer contacts with the deceased in the Spirit World; and provide a variety of healing services for the body, mind, and spirit. Staff at the Cassadaga Camp Bookstore can put visitors in touch with on-call mediums in the area and even provide a phone to make appointments.

⊚ Off map • Cassadaga Camp Bookstore, 1112 Stevens St • Open 10am–5:30pm Mon–Sat, noon–5:30pm Sun.

6 Manatee Seeker River Tour

These two-hour, pontoon-boat cruises specialize in safely allowing visitors a closer look at endangered manatees *(see p33)*. Sightings of these gentle creatures are most frequent from late October to late March, but year round, expect to see wildlife such as alligators, bald eagles, snakes, deer, and more. ⊚ *Just west of Deland on Hwy 44 at the St. John's River • Off map • Tours at 10am, 12:30pm, 3pm daily • Adm*

7 Katie's Wekiva River Landing

Discover the natural beauty of unspoiled Florida. This friendly, operation offers lodging *(see p149)*, boating, bike trails, and other outdoor pursuits in and around the Little Wekiva River. Canoes are available for rental, giving plenty of time to explore, see some of the local wildlife, and get a tan. ⊚ *190 Katie's Cove, Sanford • Off map • 407-628-1482*

8 Rivership Romance

Operating out of historic Sanford, this 1946-built triple-decked boat offers daily "eco-dining" cruises along the scenic St. John's River. It's a truly civilized way to catch a glimpse of the Florida that tourists rarely see. ⊚ *433 N. Palmetto Ave • 1-800-423-7401 • Adm • No DA*

9 Central Florida Zoological Park

Beneath this zoo's dense canopy of foliage, visitors can observe the residents

Local architecture, Mount Dora

(from howler monkeys to bald eagles, llamas, and zebu) at close quarters. Some areas fall short – the pacing big cats obviously need bigger cages – but on the whole, this makes for a rewarding trip. ⊚ *3755 N.W. Hwy 17–92, Lake Monroe • Off map • Open 9am–5pm daily • Adm*

10 Mount Dora

Just 25 miles (40 km) from Orlando, charming Mount Dora seems plucked from the 1950s. The cozy downtown is unmarred by strip malls or chain stores. Instead, the local industry is antiques, with dozens of small shops on and around Donnelly Street as well as Reninger's Antique & Flea Markets *(see p67)* on the edge of town. Train buffs can enjoy a ride on the restored *Cannonball*, a 1913 steam engine, and Lake Dora offers plenty of boating opportunities. ⊚ *Tourist info • Off map • 1-352-383-2165*

AROUND TOWN

ORLANDO'S TOP 10

Left **Lake Buena Vista** Right **Lake Buena Vista environs**

Walt Disney World® Resort & Lake Buena Vista

THERE WAS ONLY ONE *drawback to California's Disneyland, Walt Disney's first theme park, which opened in 1955: the area was prime real estate and there was no free space around the park in which to expand. So, following an aerial tour of Central Florida in 1965, Disney began covertly to buy large tracts of land. At the time, this patch of the Sunshine State was little more than cow pastures, citrus groves, and swamps, and was of little interest to anyone. Today, the 27,400-acre- (11,100-ha) Walt Disney World Resort is a self-contained and virtually self-governing entity (call 911 here and you get a Disney employee) containing four major theme parks, three water parks, several smaller attractions, and many hotels and resorts, which also spill over into the adjoining Lake Buena Vista area. For some of the 43 million guests who visit annually, it's a once-in-a-lifetime vacation, but many can't get enough of this enchanted fantasyland and return time and again to relive the experience.*

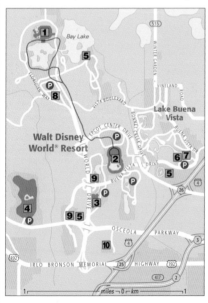

🔟 Sights

1. Magic Kingdom
2. Epcot
3. Disney-MGM Studios
4. Disney's Animal Kingdom Park
5. Water Parks
6. Cirque du Soleil
7. DisneyQuest
8. Richard Petty Driving Experience
9. Fantasia Gardens & Winter Summerland Miniature Golf
10. Disney's Wide World of Sports

1 Magic Kingdom
Who's the leader of the theme-park pack? Disney's first Florida park is the most popular in the US. *See pp8–11.*

2 Epcot
Walt Disney's guys knew something had to appeal to curious adults and techno kids. Epcot is that something. *See pp12–15.*

3 Disney-MGM Studios
A park that combines front-of-house fun with behind-the-scenes explanation. *See pp16–17.*

4 Disney's Animal Kingdom Park
Disney's fourth Orlando park is a place where elusive animals roam. *See pp18–19.*

5 Water Parks
Disney World has three water parks. The hugely popular Typhoon Lagoon, designed to resemble a beach resort devastated by a tropical storm, can hold more than 7,000 people at once, and has plenty of rides and attractions. Blizzard Beach's theme is a ski resort that melted and is a favorite among water slide fans, while River Country – Disney's original (and smallest) water park – resembles an old-fashioned swimming hole. It is usually the least crowded of the three and has the added attraction of nature trails. The parks have seasonal opening hours, so call to check. ◊ *Typhoon Lagoon • Map G2 • 407-824-2222 • Adm* ◊ *Blizzard Beach • Map G1 • 407-560-7660 • Adm* ◊ *River Country • Map F1–G2 • 407-824-222 • Adm • No DA*

6 Cirque du Soleil
Nowadays, circuses without animals are all the rage, and the Canadian company Cirque du Soleil is one of the best of its kind. So popular are its shows that, in addition to world tours, there are now permanent venues, too. Orlando's high-energy, 90-minute show, La Nouba, climaxes with a finale in which more than 70 performers execute an extraordinary trampoline routine. The ticket is quite pricey, but you're unlikely to be disappointed. ◊ *Downtown Disney West Side • Map G2 • 407-939-7600 • Shows at 6 & 9pm Thu–Mon • Adm*

Blizzard Beach

For information on Disney sights and attractions, including up-to-date hours of operation, call 407-934-7639.

89

Walt Disney

Walter Elias Disney was just 26 years old when his most famous cartoon character, Mickey Mouse, was introduced in the film *Steamboat Willie* (1928). Despite escalating success in the film world as he embraced first sound then technicolor, Disney had his sights set on more than just animation. He was the man who created the theme park, which he envisaged as a kind of 3-D movie where each individual could spin his or her own story in a totally safe, controlled, and upbeat evironment. His first, California's Disneyland Park, was the perfect vehicle for bringing Disney's clean-living family values and nostalgia for tradition to the masses. It was also the only one of his parks that came to fruition before his death in 1966 from lung cancer, 11 years after it opened.

7 DisneyQuest

This interactive, indoor theme park is divided into four zones and entertains adults as much as it does kids. Highlights of the Explore Zone include Pirates of the Caribbean: Battle for Buccaneer Gold, and Aladdin's Magic Carpet Ride. The former puts you on the deck of a two-master schooner to play cat-and-mouse with foul-mouthed pirates and foul-smelling sea monsters. Aladdin's Magic Carpet involves wearing a virtual reality helmet and taking a ride through the 3-D Cave of Wonders in search of the genie. In the Score Zone, it's all about testing your game-playing skills. Don't miss the Extraterrestrial Alien Encounter where you get to fly a space ship and blast gigantic robots, or the Mighty Ducks Pinball Slam, a life-size, sure-fire hit for pinball fans. The Create Zone unleashes the designer within:

build your own roller coaster (and then ride it in a simulator), or take a short course in cartooning at the Animation Academy. The Replay Zone is fillod with games where for an extra charge, you can win tickets that can be redeemed for prizes you can live without. Come early; crowds are worse after lunch. ❧ *Downtown Disney West Side • Map G2 • 407-828-4600 • Open 10:30am–midnight daily • Adm*

8 Richard Petty Driving Experience

Ever wanted to drive one of those souped-up, 600-horsepower NASCAR race cars, or even just be a co-pilot? Well, here's your chance to try for your dream – and a new land-speed record. The two-page waiver form that riders need to sign may shake your nerve, but there's nothing virtual about this attraction. There are two options: ride or drive. For the first, take the passenger seat while a professional drives off around the track at 145 mph (233 kmph); minimum age for this option is 16. Alternatively, spend a few hours or (if you have lots of cash to spare) days learning how to drive, and then race others for up to 30 laps (minimum age is 18 years). ❧ *Walt Disney World Speedway • Map F1 • 407-939-0130 • Opening times vary • Adm*

9 Fantasia Gardens & Winter Summerland Miniature Golf

Orlando in general and Walt Disney World Resort in particular have some great golf courses *(see pp54–5)*, but not everyone likes to take the game so seriously, or has the makings of a pro. These two miniature golf courses offer a total of 72 holes of putting fun. Inspired by the classic Disney cartoon, *Fantasia*, Fantasia Gardens' 18

Richard Petty Driving Experience

holes have an animal theme. Located near Disney-MGM Studios, it's the more forgiving of the two courses, and so the best choice for young kids or beginners. Winter Summerland is a scale model of a large course, complete with bunkers, water hazards, frustrating putting greens, and holes that are up to 75 ft (23 m) long. Choose between the winter and summer themed courses. ◎ *Fantasia Gardens • Map G2 • Open 10am–11pm daily • 407-560-8760 • Adm* ◎ *Winter Summerland • Map G1 • 407-560-3000 • Open 10am–11pm daily • Adm*

10 Disney's Wide World of Sports

Disney's sports complex is the spring training home of Major League baseball's Atlanta Braves (Feb–Mar) and minor league baseball's Orlando Rays, a farm team for the Tampa Bay Devil Rays (Apr–Sep). It's also a winter home for basketball's Harlem Globetrotters. Other facilities in the 200-acre (80-ha) complex, which is used for all kinds of amateur sports and athletics,

include: a fitness center; basketball, volleyball, and tennis courts; softball, soccer, and lacrosse fields; a martial-arts venue; and a golf-driving range. Disney's Wide World of Sports is also the home of the NFL Experience *(see p56)*. An extreme sports area catering for skateboarders, in-line skaters, and cyclists is scheduled to open at the end of 2002. ◎ *Map G2 • 407-939-1500 • Opening times vary • Adm*

Hidden Mickeys

Hidden Mickeys started many years ago as a joke among park designers. Today they're a Disney tradition. They're images of the world's most famous mouse: silhouettes of Mickey's ears, his head and ears or his whole body, semi-hidden throughout the parks and resorts. They can be any-where: in the landscaping, in the murals you pass while waiting in ride lines, and even overhead, for example on the Earffel Tower in Disney-MGM Studios. See how many you can spot (www.hiddenmickeys.com).

For more on sports and activities **See pp56–7**

Disney's BoardWalk

🔟 Best Shops

1 Yong Feng Shangdian Department Store

Here's an excellent source for all things Asian, from jade figurines to silk robes, and inlaid mother-of-pearl furnishings to wind chimes. ✥ *China Pavilion, World Showcase, Epcot • Map G2 • Adm*

2 Casbah Marketplace

Hand-tied Berber rugs, camel-bone boxes, and more are on offer in this square, which has the bustle but not the hustle of the real thing. ✥ *Morocco Pavilion, World Showcase, Epcot • Map G2 • Adm*

3 LEGO Imagination Center

Kids love the play area, which has enough LEGO pieces to build almost anything. Inside, the cash registers sing as parents buy the latest Lego gadgets. ✥ *Downtown Disney Marketplace • Map G2*

4 Mitsukoshi Department Store

An amazing selection of kimonos, samurai swords, bonsais, Japanese Disneyana, and kites is sold here. ✥ *Japan Pavilion, World Showcase, Epcot • Map G2 • Adm*

5 Guitar Gallery

This showroom is crammed with 150 models of guitar (including one made of rosewood and ivory costing $25,000), catering to all budgets. ✥ *Downtown Disney West Side • Map G2*

6 Virgin Megastore

Listen to recent releases at the numerous sound stations in this store, or browse for videos and books. ✥ *Downtown Disney West Side • Map G2*

7 Art of Disney

This large gallery is one of a kind in Florida. You'll find Disney sculptures, animation cels, and other collectibles. ✥ *Downtown Disney Marketplace • Map G2*

8 Hoypoloi Gallery

This small but sensory gallery sells sculptures, ceramics, and other imaginative oddities made of metal, stone, clay, and wood. ✥ *Downtown Disney West Side • Map G2*

9 Pooh's Corner

A veritable honeypot of merchandise: you'll find watches, jewelry, dolls, and lots more related to Pooh and his crew. ✥ *Downtown Disney Marketplace • Map G2*

10 World of Disney

The folks at Disney claim this store has the largest and most unique collection of Disney character merchandise on the planet. If you're a hardcore Disney fanatic, it's easy to spend a small fortune here. ✥ *Downtown Disney Marketplace • Map G2*

Forget to buy something? Call 407-363-6200, give the item's description and where you saw it. You can probably order it by phone.

Downtown Disney

🔟 Nighttime Attractions

1 House of Blues
One of Orlando's best venues for live music with a wide variety of musical acts (see p74). ◈ Downtown Disney West Side • Map G2 • Adm

2 Disney's BoardWalk
By night, this "seaside" boardwalk is thronged with guests enjoying the buzzing vibe and some great restaurants and clubs (see p46). ◈ Map G2 • Free

3 Downtown Disney
Probably Disney's best spot for night owls, with lots of bars and clubs to choose from (see p46). ◈ Map G2 • Free to walk around

4 Mannequins Dance Palace
A hot spot for dance fans, with a revolving floor, trendy ambience, and pumping techno. ◈ Pleasure Island • Map G2 • Adm

5 8TRAX
Specializing in 1970s music, this club is often packed with a crowd ranging from twentysomethings to those who remember the decade in question. ◈ Pleasure Island • Map G2 • Adm

6 Adventurers Club
Head here for character-based improvisation and sketch-comedy shows, which can be bawdy, absurd, and even political. ◈ Pleasure Island • Map G2 • Adm

7 Rock N Roll Beach Club
The three-story Beach Club was once a roller rink. Now it's where rock fans do their thing, drinking beers amid the video games and pool tables. A DJ and earnest cover band provide the entertainment. ◈ Pleasure Island • Map G2 • Adm

8 Pleasure Island
Apart from its clubs, this spot also boasts a freewheeling street party with DJs, food kiosks, entertainment, open-air bars, and few restrictions about drinking in public (use plastic cups). Fireworks round off the fun. ◈ Map G2 • Adm

9 Atlantic Dance Hall
This glorious 1930s-style dance hall has been re-imagined as a predominantly Latin hotspot, with a live Latin band (Thu–Sat) and a Latin DJ who spins tunes (Tue). ◈ Disney's BoardWalk • Map G2 • Closed Tue & Wed • Adm

10 Chip 'n' Dale's Campfire Sing-A-Long
Enjoy songs and marshmallows around a campfire, which are followed by a different Disney movie every night. It is open to all – just park at the River Country entrance and take the bus to the party. ◈ Meadow Trading Post, Fort Wilderness Campground • Map G2 • Free • 8pm (summer), 7pm (rest of the year)

Guests must be 21 or over to get into clubs and bars in Orlando, and need to have picture ID (driving license or passport) to prove it.

California Grill

TOP10 Resort Area Restaurants

1 Victoria & Albert's
This romantic gem has a 5-star, international menu, which is served by staff dressed as Victoria and Albert. ◎ *Disney's Grand Floridian Resort & Spa • Map F1 • 407-939-7707 • Pre-arrange vegetarian entrees • Smoke-free • No kids menu • $$$$$*

2 California Grill
One of Disney's most vegetarian-friendly restaurants offers delicious California cuisine in this romantic 15th-floor space. ◎ *Disney's Contemporary Resort • Map F1 • 407-824-1576 • Smoke-free • $$$$$*

3 Pebbles Restaurant
One of a small chain serving a creative menu that can include lamb chops with goat's cheese or beef tenderloin cooked in Ybor Gold beer. ◎ *12551 Apopka-Vineland Rd • Map F2 • 407-827-1111 • $$$$*

4 Jiko – The Cooking Place
This restaurant features a show kitchen and an inventive menu: banana-leaf steamed sea bass is a typical dish. ◎ *Disney's Animal Kingdom Lodge • Map G1 • 407-939-3463 • Smoke-free • $$$$*

5 Artist Point
Bison rib-eye steak and nut-and-herb crusted lamb chops are a few of the delicious options here. There's patio dining as well. ◎ *Disney's Wilderness Lodge • Map F1 • 407-824-1081 • Smoke-free • $$$$*

6 'Ohana
Polynesian rhythms, dancers, and storytellers provide the backdrop for this grilled meat, seafood, and all-the-trimmings buffet feast. ◎ *Disney's Polynesian Resort • Map F1 • 407-824-2000 • Smoke-free • $$$*

7 Arthur's 27
The French-style food doesn't always live up to the high prices, but the view of Disney's fireworks *(see p70)* is a winner. ◎ *Wyndham Palace Resort • Map F2 • 407-827-3450 • Pre-arrange vegetarian entrees • Smoke-free • No kids' menu • $$$$$*

8 Romano's Macaroni Grill
The pizzas and pasta comes in huge portions at this fine Italian eatery. Opera singers sometimes entertain. ◎ *12148 Apopka-Vineland Rd • Map F2 • 407-239-6676 • $$*

9 Wolfgang Puck's Café
Grilled pizza, spicy tuna rolls, and pumpkin risotto are some of the eclectic options made here by the acclaimed California chef. ◎ *Downtown Disney West Side • Map G2 • 407-938-9653 • Smoke-free • $$$*

10 Portobello Yacht Club Restaurant
This classy eatery is sure to please with thin crust pizzas, pastas, and Italian food such as slow-roasted pork loin. ◎ *Downtown Disney • Map G2 • 407-934-8888 • Smoke-free • $$$$$*

Unless stated, all restaurants advise reservations, take credit cards, and have DA, smoking tables, kids' menus, A/C, and vegetarian dishes.

Price Categories

For a three course meal for one with half a bottle of wine (or equivalent meal), taxes and extra charges.

$	under $20
$$	$20–$30
$$$	$30–$45
$$$$	$45–$60
$$$$$	over $60

Coral Reef

🔟 Theme Park Restaurants

1 Marrakesh
The seafood *bastilla* (pastry filled with fish, shrimp, mushroom, vermicelli, onion, and egg) is heavenly. Garlicky lemon chicken ranks a close second. ◈ *Morocco Pavilion, Epcot • Map G2 • 407-827-5330 • $$$$*

2 Rainforest Café
American cuisine inspired by Mexican, Carribean, and Asian flavors is served in an indoor rainforest setting. If you don't like volume and kids, this isn't for you. ◈ *Disney's Animal Kingdom • Map G1 • 407-938-9100 • Park adm not required • $$*

3 Coral Reef
Classical music and aquarium visuals are the setting here. Try the roasted snapper with veggies. ◈ *Living Seas Pavilion, Epcot • Map G2 • 407-939-3463 • $$$$*

4 Cinderella's Royal Table
This restaurant in a castle has a great menu, with tasty prime-rib pastry-pie leading the way. ◈ *Fantasyland, Magic Kingdom • Map F1 • 407-939-3463 • Pre-arrange vegetarian entrees • No alcohol • $$$$*

5 Akershus
Hunker down for traditional Norweigian dishes (herring, potato salad, gravlax in mustard sauce, venison stew, and more) in a medieval castle setting. ◈ *Norway Pavilion, Epcot • Map G2 • 407-939-3463 • $$$*

6 Hollywood Brown Derby
Polish off SoCal dishes such as skillet-seared tuna with the signature grapefruit cake with cream-cheese icing. ◈ *Disney-MGM Studios • Map G2 • 407-939-3463 • Pre-arrange vegetarian entrees • $$$*

7 San Angel Inn
Try *mole poblano* (chicken with spices and chocolate) or beef with black beans and fried plantain at this south-of-the-border eatery. ◈ *Mexico Pavilion, Epcot • Map G2 • 407-827-8558 • $$$*

8 Rose & Crown Pub & Dining Room
A pub-grub joint offering British staples such as bangers and mash, rib with Yorkshire pudding, and Cornish pasties. ◈ *UK Pavilion, Epcot • Map G2 • 407-939-3463 • Pre-arrange vegetarian entrees • $$$*

9 Chefs de France
Three French chefs created this brasserie-style restaurant full of Gallic flare and flavor. ◈ *France Pavilion, Epcot • Map G2 • 407-939-3463 • Pre-arrange vegetarian entrees • $$$$*

10 Liberty Tree Tavern
Buffet-style American fare, such as roasted turkey, flank steak, and ham, is served in a colonial setting. ◈ *Liberty Sq, Magic Kingdom • Map F1 • 407-939-3463 • Pre-arrange vegetarian entrees • No alcohol • $$$*

➤ *For information on Priority Seating in Walt Disney World Resort* **See p134**

Left **Wet 'n Wild** Right **Universal Studios**

International Drive Area

CONSIDERED THE TIMES SQUARE OF *Orlando*, International Drive is a brash 10-mile (16-km) strip boasting five theme parks, countless attractions open day and night, including Universal's CityWalk entertainment complex, and the USA's second-largest convention center. Added to the mix are hundreds of hotels and resorts catering to all budgets, shopping malls and outlet stores, and themed and fast-food restaurants. As a package, the result is a frenetic zone, which, despite its wall-to-wall neon signs and visual overload, has become a serious competitor of Disney World, appealing to visitors who prefer to stay away from the clutches of Mickey but want to be in the thick of the action.

CityWalk, Universal Orlando

Sights & Attractions

1. Islands of Adventure
2. Universal Studios Florida
3. Wet 'n Wild
4. SeaWorld Orlando
5. Discovery Cove
6. Fun Spot Action Park
7. Ripley's Believe It or Not! Odditorium
8. Holy Land Experience
9. WonderWorks
10. Titanic – Ship of Dreams

Islands of Adventure

1 Islands of Adventure
Few visitors would contest the claim of this Universal park to being king of the Orlando thrill-ride circuit. See pp20–23.

2 Universal Studios Florida
Part studio and part attraction, the movie-themed rides and shows here really let visitors step inside the movies. See pp24–7.

3 Wet 'n Wild
It's hard to out-do Disney, but Wet 'n Wild is arguably Orlando's best sun-and-swim water park attraction, with plenty of slides and rides to amuse. See pp34–5.

4 SeaWorld Orlando
Anheuser-Busch's Orlando outpost offers animal attractions and a refreshing change of pace to the fast rides and cartoon characters overrunning the other parks. See pp28–31.

5 Discovery Cove
You might be in land-locked Orlando, but you can still fulfil those tropical island fantasies of swimming with dolphins and snorkeling over coral reefs if you check in to Discovery Cove. The dolphin swim is the biggest draw (each session lasts about one hour), but the white-sand beaches, snorkeling opportunities in fresh and salt-water lagoons, and soothing beach-resort vibe elicits just as much praise. Admission is not cheap (largely because there are never more than 1,000 visitors daily), but you get almost everything you need for the day thrown in, including sun block, lunch, and snorkel gear, as well as a seven-day pass to SeaWorld. This secluded oasis is not for everyone – kids might miss the lack of thrill rides – but for a unique beach escape that doesn't require leaving Orlando, this is the place. ✆ 6000 Discovery Cove Way • Map T6 • 407-370-1280 • Open 8:30am–5:30pm daily • Adm

Discovery Cove

6 Fun Spot Action Park
This arcade-cum-amusement-park has something for everyone who has a little bit of the child in them. The park has four go-kart tracks, with corkscrew and banked turns, 30-degree descents, bridges, and more. In addition, there are bumper boats and cars, a 100-ft (30-m) Ferris wheel, 100 arcade games, and a kid zone that has swings, a train, spinning tea cups, and flying bears. ✆ 5551 Del Verde Way, Orlando • Map U2 • 407-363-3867 • 10am–9pm daily, sometimes later • Free (but ride and game prices vary) • Min age for solo go-karting is 10 yrs

Fun Spot Action Park

Ripley's Believe It or Not! Odditorium

7 Ripley's Believe It or Not! Odditorium

If you're a fan of the bizarre, you'll love Ripley's. This worldwide chain of attractions displays the unbelievable finds of Robert Ripley's 40 years of adventures, the reports of which were published in more than 300 newspapers and read by more than 80 million people. The Orlando branch has a full-scale model of a 1907 Silver Ghost Rolls Royce (with moving engine parts) built out of 1,016,711 match sticks and 63 pints (36 l) of glue; a flute made of human bones; a mosaic of the Mona Lisa made out of toast; shrunken heads; a five-legged cow; and a portrait of Van Gogh made from 3,000 postcards. You'll also encounter a holographic 1,069-lb- (485-kg) man, plus films of strange feats such as people swallowing coat-hangers. ⓢ *8201 International Dr • Map T3 • 407-363-4418 • Open 9–1am daily • Adm*

The Peabody Ducks

Their existence came about because of a practical joke, but now these five mallards, which reside in the Peabody Hotel *(see p143)*, are among the best known and most unusual celebrities in I-Drive. As befits VIPs (Very Important Poultry), they spend much of each day in their $100,000 glass-enclosed home, called the 'Duck Palace'. But what draws the crowds is their twice daily procession (at 11am and 5pm), when they waddle through the hotel lobby, led by their own red-coated duck master, on the way to and from the lobby fountain.

8 Holy Land Experience

Marvin J. Rosenthal, a Christian convert and Baptist minister, created quite a stir when he opened this religious theme park in 2001. Set in a half-scale reconstruction of the Temple of the Great King, which stood in Jerusalem in the 1st century AD, the park aims to take visitors 7,000 miles (11,200 km) away and 3,000 years back to the ancient Jerusalem of biblical times (BC 1450 to AD 66 to be exact). The attraction has models of the limestone caves where the Dead Sea Scrolls were discovered and Jesus's tomb. It also has displays of rare antiquated Bibles and biblical manuscripts, an outdoor stage where actors portraying biblical personalities tell stories from the Old and New Testaments, and a café that serves Middle Eastern food. ⓢ *4655 Vineland Rd • Map D4 • 407-872-2272 • Open 9:30am–7pm, sometimes later, Mon–Sat; noon–6pm Sun • Adm*

Holy Land Experience

WonderWorks
9 You can't miss this attraction from the outside: it looks as though a classical building has landed upside down on top of a warehouse. Inside, there are 85 hands-on exhibits. Highlights include an earthquake simulator; a Bridge of Fire, where you can literally experience the hair-raising effects of 250,000 watts

WonderWorks

of static electricity; and Virtual Hoops, which uses some of the latest cinema technology to put you on TV to play basketball against one of the NBA's top players. You can also try Virtual Hang Gliding, which sends you soaring like a bird through the Grand Canyon, and WonderCoaster, which challenges your roller coaster-designing skills and then your nerve to ride your creation in a simulator. WonderWorks also runs a laser-tag venue and a twice-nightly magic show, both of which cost extra. ◈ *Pointe Orlando, 9067 International Dr • Map T4 • 407-351-8800 • Open 9am–midnight daily • Adm*

Titanic – Ship of Dreams

Titanic – Ship of Dreams
10 This exhibit's 200 artifacts include a real life jacket and an old deck chair, which were both recovered from the wreckage of the fateful liner, as well as the Titanic's second-class passenger list. The attraction also has full-scale re-creations of some of the ship's rooms, including its grand staircase, as well as memorabilia from three major Titanic movies – including one of the costumes worn by Leonardo DiCaprio. Actors in period garb play out events that occured on the fateful journey, telling the story of the White Star Line's supposedly unsinkable ship. Most of the artifacts came out of private collections from both the United Kingdom and the USA. ◈ *The Mercado, 8445 International Dr • Map T3 • 407-248-1166 • Open 10am–9pm daily • Adm*

I-Ride Trolley
One of the best things about I-Drive itself is the tourist-oriented I-Ride Trolley, which offers an easy way to ogle some of the area's oddities and its high-density visual overload. It is also an excellent and extremely cheap way to get around this part of town while avoiding the need to get involved in fighting I-Drive's frustratingly heavy traffic, or walking any distance in the heat. There are 46 stops on the circuit, serving all the local major attractions, shopping malls, hotels, and restaurants. *See p127.*

Left **Between the Buns** Center **Skull Kingdom** Right **Sports Dominator**

Eye-Openers on I-Drive

1 Sheraton Studio City Hotel
A most distinctive 21-story circular hotel with an interior Deco-inspired design and lighting theme. ⊛ 5905 International Dr • Map T2

2 Skull Kingdom
Like a backdrop in an old horror movie, this funhouse takes the form of a spooky castle atop a giant skull. It's even better lit up at night. ⊛ 5933 American Way • Map T2

3 Florida Celebration Gift Shop
A replica of the space shuttle is bolted to the façade of this gift shop, which is actually completely unrelated to space exploration. ⊛ 6328 International Dr • Map T2

4 Bargain World
The doorway to this shop is straddled by a large flying saucer. Alighting from a nearby rocket-ship is a giant green Martian wearing casual clothes and holding a stick – no doubt to root out those bargains. ⊛ 6464 International Dr • Map T2

5 Sports Dominator
Giant, stern-faced effigies of sports people flank the entrance to this store. One muscle-bound guy wearing tight pants looks like a reject from the Village People. ⊛ 6464 International Dr • Map T2

6 Between the Buns
Some describe it as an example of form-follows-function Programmatic architecture from the 1920s. Others just see it as a 25-ft- (8-m) long frankfurter. ⊛ 6600 International Dr • Map T2

7 Ripley's Believe It or Not! Odditorium
This place is built to look as if one of Florida's sinkholes opened up and nearly swallowed the building. See p98.

8 Guinness World Records Experience
Geometric minimalism is not common on I-Drive, but the architecture at this testament to man's endeavors is an exception to the rule. ⊛ 8437 International Dr • Map T3

9 WonderWorks
As the marketing story goes, a tornado picked up this four-story building and sent it crashing upside down on top of a 1930s era brick warehouse. Silly perhaps, but it stops traffic. See p99.

10 FAO Schwarz
As if a gigantic toy box had been upended, FAO Schwarz is surrounded by a jumble of huge playthings, including colorful blocks that spell out the store's name. See p101.

For tips on shopping in Orlando See p132

Left **Edwin Watts Golf National Clearance Center** Right **FAO Schwarz**

🔟 I-Drive Stores & Outlet Centers

1 Nike Factory Store
A gigantic collection of all things adorned with the famous "swoosh," at discount prices. ✪ *Belz Factory Outlet World, 5201 W. Oak Ridge Rd • Map U1*

2 Kenneth Cole
Choose from recent lines of urbane Cole shoes; handbags, clothing, and accessories also vie for attention. Expect savings of at least 25 per cent. ✪ *Belz Designer Outlet Center, 5211 International Dr • Map U1*

3 FAO Schwarz
Not only is this store bursting at the seams with all kinds of toys, but kids are allowed to play with almost everything. ✪ *Pointe Orlando, 9101 International Dr • Map T4*

4 Bass Pro Shops Outdoor World
Overflowing with fishing, golf, camping, and hunting supplies, plus footwear and apparel, this is a vast shrine to the great outdoors. ✪ *5156 International Dr • Map U1*

5 Coach Factory Store
Leather rules at this spacious store, and deals abound on both current and last season's handbags, jackets, luggage, and more. ✪ *Belz Designer Outlet Center, 5269 International Dr • Map U1*

6 Edwin Watts Golf National Clearance Center
Like cars, golf clubs also have model years. This store offers last season's hot drivers and putters at deep savings. ✪ *8330 International Dr • Map T3*

7 Brooks Brothers Outlet
The suit selection here is slim, but there's a great range of current-season casual sportswear for men and women, discounted by at least 40 per cent. ✪ *Belz Designer Outlet Center, 5247 International Dr • Map U1*

8 Off 5th
Like Sak's Fifth Avenue's regular stores, this outlet is heavy on high fashion, packed with brand names, and has a rapid merchandise turnover. ✪ *Belz Designer Outlet Center, 5253 International Dr • Map U1*

9 Fossil Company Store
The impulse-buy watches at Fossil are cheap, fun, and have a pop-culture aesthetic. ✪ *Belz Designer Outlet Center, 5229 International Dr • Map U1*

10 Divers Direct Outlet
This deep discount outlet carries everything needed for underwater adventures. The sales team is good at giving advice, so don't hesitate to ask for help. ✪ *5403 International Dr • Map U1*

Most stores on I-Drive are open 10am–10pm Mon–Sat and noon–6pm Sun.

Left **CityJazz** Right **Hard Rock Live**

Bars, Clubs, & Entertainment

1 Hard Rock Live
One of the best spots in town to see live music (national and local rock and R&B acts), with a top-notch sound system. ⊚ *CityWalk • Map T1 • Adm*

2 The Groove
This powerhouse dance club has slamming DJs, as well as several quiet chill-out lounges. ⊚ *CityWalk • Map T1 • Adm • Over 21 yrs*

3 XS Orlando
Orlando's ultimate games room is on the second floor of this entertainment mecca, offering DJs, bars, food, and more than 110 of the latest interactive games. Their motto? "Too much is not enough." ⊚ *Pointe Orlando, 9101 International Dr • Map T4 • Free*

4 Metropolis
The DJ plays 1980s and '90s sounds and there are seven billiard tables at this glitzy venue. ⊚ *Pointe Orlando, 9101 International Dr • 407-370-3700 • Map T4 • Adm after 10pm • Over 21 yrs*

5 Matrix
This new club pumps out house and electronica to a young, vibrant crowd. ⊚ *Pointe Orlando, 9101 International Dr • Map T4 • Adm • Over 18 yrs (women), over 21 yrs (men) • DA*

6 Latin Quarter
Expect anything Latin – from food to dance lessons – at this energetic venue. A 13-piece Latin band is on most nights. ⊚ *CityWalk • Map T1 • Adm after 10pm Thu–Sat*

7 Adobe Gilas
Crowds of 20-somethings swarm this restaurant/bar (boasting 65 varieties of tequila) and dance the night away to cover bands. ⊚ *Pointe Orlando, 9101 International Dr • Map T4 • Free • DA*

8 Bob Marley – A Tribute To Freedom
Live outdoor reggae music is the big draw here, and the bands are often excellent. ⊚ *CityWalk • Map T1 • Over 21 yrs only after 10 pm • Occasional evening adm*

9 Cricketers Arms Pub
A little piece of England, with European soccer on the TVs, darts, and nearly 20 ales, lagers, bitters, and stouts on tap. Blues bands sometimes perform. ⊚ *Mercado, 8445 International Dr • Map T3 • Free*

10 CityJazz
This beautiful and acoustically vibrant room emulates the big, urbane jazz supper clubs of the past. ⊚ *CityWalk • Map T1 • Occasional adm*

Around Town – International Drive Area

Age restrictions (18 or 21 years) for shows and clubs vary. Bring your photo ID to make sure you are not turned away at the door.

Price Categories

For a three course meal for one with half a bottle of wine (or equivalent meal), taxes, and extra charges.

$	under $20
$$	$20–$30
$$$	$30–$45
$$$$	$45–$60
$$$$$	over $60

Ran-Getsu of Tokyo

🔟 Places to Eat

1 Café Tu Tu Tango
Local artists' work adorns the walls of this vaguely Latin-style eatery. Dishes include black bean soup, shrimp fritters, and quesadillas. ✎ *8625 International Dr • Map T3 • 407-248 2222 • $$*

2 Ran-Getsu of Tokyo
High-class Japanese tourists endorse Ran-Getsu's authenticity, and enjoy dishes ranging from sushi to teriyaki. ✎ *8400 International Dr • Map T4 • 407-345-0044 • $$$$*

3 Roy's
On the menu here are Hawaiian fusion dishes such as sesame-oil-seared mahi-mahi with red Thai curry sauce. ✎ *7760 W. Sand Lake Rd • S3 • 407-352-4844 • Smoke-free • $$$$*

4 Siam Orchid
Orlando's No. 1 Thai restaurant, due in part to the owners' insistence on using fresh herbs and authentic recipes.
✎ *7575 Universal Dr • Map T3 • 407-351-0821 • Smoke-free • No kids' menu • $$$$*

5 Atlantis
Expect the bluesy feel of a 1930s supper club and dishes such as a seafood medley, and pan-seared duck. ✎ *Orlando Renaissance SeaWorld Resort, 6677 Sea Harbour Dr • Map T5 • 407-351-5555 • No kids' menu • $$$$*

6 Christini's
This place is popular with visiting celebrities, attracted by a menu that includes sage-seasoned veal and cognac-cured shrimp. ✎ *7600 Dr. Phillips Blvd • Map S3 • 407-345-8770 • No kids' menu • $$$$$*

7 Delfino Riviera
Feast on upscale Italian delights such as monkfish with black-olive pasta and lobster-champagne risotto. ✎ *Portofino Bay Hotel, Universal Orlando • Map T1 • 407-503-3463 • Pre-arrange vegetarian dishes • Smoke-free • $$$$$*

8 Bahama Breeze
Trust the Caribbean menu and spirits to create some fun, but expect to wait up to two hours for a table. ✎ *8849 International Dr • Map T4 • 407-248-2499 • no reservations • $$*

9 Chili's Grill & Bar
One of the better chains offering Tex-Mex food including fajitas, sandwiches, and grills, with low-fat options. ✎ *7021 International Dr • T2 • 407-352-7618 • $$*

10 The Palm
Think high-end steaks, often belly-busters (up to a 36-oz [1.2-kg] strip for two) but don't overlook the lobster option. ✎ *Hard Rock Hotel, 5800 Universal Blvd • Map T1 • 407-503-7256 • $$$$$*

➡ *Unless stated, all restaurants advise reservations, take credit cards, and have DA, smoking tables, kids' menus, A/C, and vegetarian dishes.*

Left **Osceola County Historical Museum & Pioneer Center** Right **Gatorland**

Kissimmee

WHAT USED TO BE A COW TOWN *has in the past few decades evolved into an inexpensive hotel enclave for Disney World tourists. But there's more to Kissimmee than cheap places to sleep. Though U.S. 192 (also called the Irlo Bronson Memorial Highway) is dense with strip malls and hotels – and looks like a grim vision of tourist hell – downtown Kissimmee (centered on Broadway and Emmet streets) was built in the early 1890s and boasts attractive low-slung buildings, which house several antique and gift shops. The land surrounding U.S. 192 is relatively undeveloped, providing Kissimmee visitors with easy access to Florida's rich, natural beauty. A terrific variety of outdoor pursuits is available to the visitor who is willing to spend time away from the theme parks.*

Downtown Kissimmee

Sights & Attractions

1 Gatorland
2 Celebration
3 World of Orchids
4 Osceola County Historical Museum & Pioneer Center
5 Green Meadows Petting Farm
6 Water Mania Water Park
7 Old Town
8 Splendid China
9 Flying Tigers Warbird Restoration Museum
10 Kissimmee Rodeo

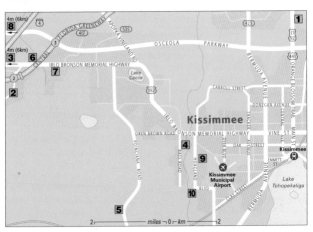

World of Orchids

Gatorland
Gatorland, Orlando's original theme park, opened more than 50 years ago as a swampy roadside stand, and is now home to well over 1,000 alligators, crocodiles, and snakes. Its appeal? A chance to gaze, just steps away from these mysterious creatures, who remain curiously similar to their prehistoric relatives. Visitors can stroll along a boardwalk over lakes full of cranky gators and buy hot dogs to throw into their mouths. A bizarre and unique attraction. ⊗ 14501 S. Orange Blossom Trail • Map G4 • Open 9am–6pm daily • Adm

Celebration
When Walt Disney conceived of Epcot (see pp12–15), he imagined it as a residential community happily engaged in road-testing futuristic technologies. After his death, that dream went out the window only to resurface years later here. However, instead of looking to the future, Celebration salutes the past in a cliché of small town USA (think The Truman Show). The houses are pretty, the downtown has some good restaurants and a cinema, and everything is upscale. This is not an attraction, but it is quite a sight. ⊗ Located E. of I-4 at Exit 25. Turn right at Celebration Ave and follow the signs • Map G2

World of Orchids
This unusual and serene spot was founded in 1983 by a couple who moved north when their Miami orchid nursery was destroyed by Hurricane Andrew. There are more than 1,000 orchids on display in the conservatory and outside on the nature walk, both of which are densely and beautifully landscaped. ⊗ 2501 Old Lake Wilson Rd • Map H1 • Open 9:30am–4:30pm Tue–Sun • Free

Osceola County Historical Museum & Pioneer Center
This homespun outdoor museum gives a glimpse of Kissimmee life before Disney. The focal point is a pair of late 1800s "Cracker-style" cypress wood buildings, complete with "possum trot" breezeway – an early form of air-conditioning. One showcases a simple home, while the other is reconfigured as a general store, selling local history books, crafts, and guides for the nature preserve located across the street. ⊗ 750 N. Bass Rd • Map H3 • Open Thu–Sat 10am–4pm • Adm

Green Meadows Petting Farm
This educational spot is perfect for anyone who might enjoy milking a cow, riding a pony, getting close to more than 300 friendly farm animals, and learning a bit about them in the process. Two-hour guided tours are included with admission, and picnic facilities are available if you want to eat lunch here. ⊗ 1368 S. Poinciana Blvd • Map H3 • Open 9:30–5:30 daily • Adm

Green Meadows Petting Farm

6 Water Mania

Thirty-six acres (15 ha) of twisting, turning waterslides and plenty of places to chill out and float in an inner tube make this waterpark a particular favorite among teens and young adults. It's less themed than Disney waterparks *(see p89)*, smaller than Wet 'n Wild *(see pp34–5)*, but, unless the weather

Water Mania

is bad, usually pretty crowded. ⊗ *6073 W. Irlo Bronson Hwy • Map G2 • Open 10am–5pm daily (summer); 10am–5pm Wed–Sat (winter) • Adm*

7 Old Town

Essentially, this is a tourist-oriented shopping mall filled with around 75 stores covering the usual array of gifts, novelties, and souvenirs – kitsch or otherwise. What sets it apart from other gift shop strips are the numerous entertainment options: a cheerful 18-ride amusement park, Laser Tag, a Haunted House, carousel, live music performances, and a vintage car show every Friday and Saturday night. It's very much about family fun, and there's no charge for admission, although the carnival rides are

priced separately. On a warm Florida night, the feeling is one of strolling the bustling midway of a state fair. ⊗ *5770 W. Irlo Bronson Hwy • Map G2 • Open 10am–11pm daily • Free*

8 Splendid China

This collection of more than 60 miniature architectural attractions from China is certainly impressive, but their tiny stature makes the place look like a giant mini-golf course. With absolutely nothing in the way of roller coasters or motion simulators, the atmosphere here is decidedly low-stress, making the place popular with older visitors. There are also interesting demonstrations of Chinese crafts, a worthwhile 90-minute live show, *The Mysterious Kingdom of the Orient*, as well as an on-site gourmet Chinese restaurant, The Suzhou Pearl. ⊗ *3000 Splendid China Blvd • Map G1 • Open at 9:30am daily (closing times vary) • Adm*

9 Flying Tigers Warbird Restoration Museum

Of the tens of thousands of warplanes built between World War II and the Vietnam War, few are still around, let alone in flying condition. This museum is working to change that by painstakingly restoring a vast collection of historically important aircraft. Visitors can tour the restoration hangar, sign up for history and restoration classes, and even take the controls of a World War II

Flying Tigers Warbird Restoration Museum

Splendid China

flight trainer. Those who wish to stay earthbound can just take in the sight of the planes as they fly off. ◈ *231 N. Hoagland Blvd • Map H3 • Open 9am–5pm daily • Adm*

10 Kissimmee Rodeo

Once upon a time, before it became a suburb of Disney World, Kissimmee was part of Florida's important beef industry, and populated by cowboys (sometimes called Crackers because of the sound made by their whips). Quite a few remain in the area today, and this Friday night bash is where they celebrate the skills of Kissimmee's original cowboys. Bear in mind, this is no tourist attraction – it's a bonafide rodeo with cash prizes and real danger. Angry bulls have been known to crush the skull of an occasional unlucky cowboy. ◈ *958 S. Hoagland Blvd • Map H3 • 407-933-0020 • 8pm Fri • Adm*

Kissimmee Rodeo

A Day in Kissimmee

Morning

There are countless breakfast buffets in the area, all offering mounds of food, from fresh fruit to omelets. Find the one closest to you and start the day there. As mornings tend to be cooler and a bit less insect-ridden than afternoons, follow your meal with a self-guided tour of swamp life at **Airboat Rentals You Drive** *(see p110)*. Head as far away as possible from the the road, cut the engine, and enjoy the silence. Most of Florida used to be like this. For lunch, head to Kissimmee's historic Downtown and pop in to Azteca's (809 N. Main St), a tiny and original Tex-Mex restaurant. Be careful ordering anything "very hot"; the cook takes this as a personal challenge and will likely spice the dish so your head explodes.

Afternoon

From Downtown, it's a short drive north to **Gatorland**. The massive gators prowling the front lakes are the big attraction. But smart guests will take the Swamp Walk, check out the crocodile pens, and survey the alligator breeding marsh from the observation tower. There are four live animal shows but if time is tight, Gator Jump-A-Roo and Gator Wrestling are the essentials.

Evening

For dinner, the slightly camp **Pacino's Italian Ristorante** *(see p111)* is popular for its home-style Italian favorites and delicious pizza. Afterwards, take another short drive to **Old Town** where kids can play on the rides while adults watch from a bench enjoying an ice cream.

Around Town – Kissimmee

Left **Parasailing, Boggy Creek** Center **Fishing, Kissimmee** Right **Aquatic Wonders Boat Tours**

🔟 Leisure Pursuits & Activities

1 East Lake Fish Camp
This lakeside facility provides everything from fishing poles to boats, bait, and bunks. Large mouth bass are the stars, with game fish also hitting the lines. ⊗ *3705 Big Bass Rd • Off map • 407-348-2040 • Adm • No DA*

2 Fun With Jetskis
Here's the place to race around on one- to three-seat motorcycles for the water. ⊗ *4960 W. Irlo Bronson Memorial Hwy • Map G3 • 407-397-0906 • Adm • No DA*

3 Aquatic Wonders Boat Tours
Choose from themed tours, including gator-watching, lake ecology, and Native American constellation tales, aboard this six-passenger pontoon boat. ⊗ *101 Lakeshore Blvd • Map H4 • 407-846-2814 • Adm*

4 Airboat Rentals You Drive
After instruction, take off in a small airboat to commune with nature deep in a cypress swamp. ⊗ *4266 W. Hwy 192 • Map H3 • 407-847-3672 • Adm • No DA*

5 Osceola Center For The Arts
Here, culture mavens will find anything from theater to music events, and exhibitions. ⊗ *2411 E. Irlo Bronson Memorial Hwy • 407-846-6257 • Adm*

6 Boggy Creek Airboat Rides
These 18-passenger flat-bottomed skiffs powered by giant fans make regular daylight and special one-hour night tours. ⊗ *3702 Big Bass Rd • Off map • 407-344-9550 • Adm*

7 The Ice Factory
Get out of the Florida sun and do a few laps on this ice rink, which also has a kids' play area. ⊗ *2221 Partin Settlement Rd • Map H5 • 407-933-4259 • Adm • No DA*

8 Falcon's Fire Golf Club
This immaculately groomed public golf course is often cited as one of the best in Florida. ⊗ *3200 Seralago Blvd • Map G3 • 407-397-2777 • Adm • No DA*

9 Boggy Creek Parasail Rides
Take the chance to parasail attached to a powerboat that pulls you high above East Lake Tohopekalgia. ⊗ *3702 Big Bass Rd • Off map • 407-348-2700 • Adm • No DA*

10 Kissimmee Golf Driving Range
This venue features a flood-lit driving range with natural grass and mats, as well as an 18-hole miniature course and batting cages. ⊗ *2100 E. Irlo Bronson Memorial Hwy • Map H5 • 407-847-6502 • Adm • No DA*

For more sports & activities **See pp56–7**

Price Categories

For a three course
meal for one with half
a bottle of wine (or
equivalent meal), taxes,
and extra charges.

$	under $20
$$	$20–$30
$$$	$30–$45
$$$$	$45–$60
$$$$$	over $60

Tarantino's Italian Restaurant

⁑10 Places to Eat

1 Charley's Steak House
Charley's uses an Indian cook-ing method, yielding steaks that are charred outside, juicy inside. ◈ 2901 Parkway Blvd • Map G2 • 407-239-1270 • Closed lunch • $$$$

2 Azteca's Mexican
Authentic Mexican and Tex-Mex is served in an extravagantly decorated room. ◈ 809 N. Main St • Map H4 • 407-933-8155 • $ • No DA

3 Tarantino's Italian Restaurant
This delightful Italian spot wins praise for charming ambience and well-prepared Italian classics. ◈ Four Points Sheraton, 4018 W. Vine St • Map H3 • 407-870-2622 • Closed lunch • $$$

4 Karen's 2nd Precinct Café
A favorite with cops from the police station across the street, this cheerful café is perfect for a sandwich or salad. ◈ 17 Broadway • Map H4 • 407-944-9405 • Open lunch Mon–Fri • $ • No reservations • No kids' menu

5 Pacino's Italian Ristorante
Sicilian specialties here include hand-cut steaks, veal chops, and great pizza and pasta. ◈ 5795 W. Orlo Bronson Memorial Hwy • Map G2 • 407-396-8022 • $$$

6 Puerto Rico Café
It's a bit of a dive, but don't let that put you off trying the delicious mojo-enhanced steaks and sea-food. ◈ 507 W. Vine St • Map H4 • 407-847-6399 • Open daily • $$ • No DA

7 Pounder's Fresh Fish & Lobster House
Similar dishes to some big sea-food chains are served here, but the fare here is fresher, more varied, and tastier. ◈ 1213 N. Central Ave • Map G2 • 407-846 8980 • $$$

8 Black Angus Restaurant
Melt-in-your-mouth steaks are the focus of this award-winning, family eatery, but ribs and fried chicken are also popular. There's a great breakfast buffet, too. ◈ 2001 W. Irlo Bronson Memorial Hwy • Map H4 • 407-846-7117 • $$

9 Logan's Roadhouse
With its neon signs and country jukebox, the vibe here is 1940s, honky-tonk, roadside grill. Try the mesquite-grilled steaks or honey sweet rolls. ◈ 5925 W. Irlo Bronson Memorial Hwy • Map G2 • 407-390-0500 • $$$

10 Atlantic Bay Seafood Grill
The nautical decor is a bit kitsch, but nothing's wrong with the fish and seafood dished up here. Order it in any number of ways (including blackened). There are plenty of non-fish options, too. ◈ 12901 Parkway Blvd • Map G2 • 407-396-7736 • Closed lunch • $$$

Around Town – Kissimmee

 Unless stated, all restaurants advise reservations, take credit cards, and have DA, smoking tables, kids' menus, A/C, and vegetarian dishes. **111**

Left **Downtown Skyline** Right **Orange County Regional History Center**

Downtown Orlando

MOST FOLKS ASSUME ORLANDO IS *just about Walt Disney and amusement parks, with the odd cowboy and conservative Christian thrown in for good measure. But that's not the case. Long a state capital for the banking and citrus industries, Orlando's Downtown also contains several of the city's leading*

Orlando Science Center

museums, as well as its best-known park, a lovely green oasis that surrounds Lake Eola, which boasts dramatic skyline vistas. By day Downtown is a relaxed southern enclave, but by night it transforms into a throbbing club scene – despite the decline of the famous entertainment, dining, and shopping zone, Church Street Station. Orange Avenue is the main street and most evenings, herds of party people, both gay and straight, migrate from club to club in search of cheap drinks and hot DJs – and there are plenty of both.

🔟 Sights

1. Orlando Science Center
2. Orlando Museum of Art
3. Orange County Regional History Center
4. Harry P. Leu Gardens
5. Mennello Museum of American Folk Art
6. The Vietnamese District
7. Lake Eola Park
8. Orlando Hauntings Ghost Tours
9. Church Street
10. Colonial Lanes

1 Orlando Science Center

The workings of the natural world, from the infinitesimal to the overwhelming, are on display here. Big interactive fun awaits at the Body Zone, where a huge mouth introduces an exhibit about the digestive system. The vast Cinedome shows movies about topics such as Egyptian treasures and ocean life, and on weekend evenings, star-gazers can climb to the top floors to pick out the planets through a telescope. ⊗ *777 E. Princeton St • Map M3 • 407-514-2000 • Open 9am–5pm Tue–Thu, 9am–9pm Fri & Sat, noon–5pm Sun • Adm*

2 Orlando Museum of Art (OMA)

The focus of exhibitions in this big, bright museum is American art from the 19th century onward, art from the ancient Americas and Africa, and block-buster traveling shows. On the first Thursday evening of every month, you can also enjoy music, food, and the work of local artists for an inventively themed get-together. ⊗ *2416 N. Mills Ave • Map M3 • 407-896-4231 • 10am–5pm Tue–Sat, noon–5pm Sun • Adm*

3 Orange County Regional History Center

From the informative to the kitsch, the History Center highlights the formative periods and industries of Central Florida. Dioramas show scenes of early Native Americans, and a re-created Florida Cracker house can be inspected. There's also a display called The Day We Changed, which chronicles the impact of the arrival of the Disney theme parks. Some exhibits fall a little flat, but many elements, such as the stuffed alligators and pink flamingos, betray a sense of fun. ⊗ *65 E. Central Blvd • Map P3 • 407-836-8500 • 10am–5pm Mon–Sat, 12–5pm Sun • Adm*

Fountain, Lake Eola Park

4 Harry P. Leu Gardens

Well-tended pathways weave through this elegant 50-acre (20-ha) park. Earthy scents waft from an herb garden, while another contains plants that attract butterflies. Depending on the season, visitors might catch roses in bloom (in Florida's largest rose garden) or the grace of camellias. Guides conduct tours of the early 20th-century Leu House. ⊗ *1920 N. Forest Ave • Map M4 • 407-246-2620 • Open 9am–5pm daily • Adm*

5 Mennello Museum of American Folk Art

Half of the Mennello is devoted to the work of Florida folk artist Earl Cunningham (1893–1977), who created vibrant, whimsical pastoral paintings glowing with orange skies and yellow rivers. The other half houses traveling exhibits of folk art. The lakeside grounds contain wonderfully quirky sculptures scattered here and there. ⊗ *900 E. Princeton St • Map M3 • 407-246-4278 • 11am–5pm Mon–Sat, noon–5pm Sun • Adm*

Mennello Museum of American Folk Art

6 The Vietnamese District

This area, also known as the ViMi district (for the crossroads at Virginia and Mills avenues), is a less obvious ethnic enclave than, say, New York's Chinatown. Nevertheless, it is still clustered with Vietnamese restaurants and shops, as well as delights from other Asian countries. The thickest concentration is south of Virginia, at Colonial Drive. *Mills Ave bet Virginia Ave & Colonial Dr • Map N3*

7 Lake Eola Park

A pedestrian-only path encircles Lake Eola, offering a pleasing view of downtown's skyline. Those willing to exert their leg muscles can rent swan-shaped paddle boats *(see p47).* Real swans drift along in the lake's shallow water and will venture onto dry land if offered a handful of the food that can be bought for small change. Plays and concerts are performed at the Walt Disney Amphitheater, a bandshell with surprisingly decent acoustics. Disney's presence is more ostentatiously displayed with the rather incongruous Millennium clock located on the lake's southern side. *Map P3*

Signs, Vietnamese Disctrict

8 Orlando Hauntings Ghost Tours

A guide in 19th-century costume holds a lantern and tries his best to spook his willing participants, while leading this 90-minute walking tour. Groups of up to 25 people hear tales of murder, morbidity, and ghost sightings, and as an added bonus, the guide recounts wonderful anecdotes and information about the architecture and history of Downtown's most interesting buildings.
Depart from Guinevere's coffee house, at Pine St & Magnolia Av • Map P3 • 407-992-1200 • 6pm & 8 pm, first & third Sat of every month • Adm

9 Church Street

The stretch of Church Street that lies between Orange Avenue and I-4 is thick with enough specialty shops, restaurants, and bars to keep visitors engaged for hours. The anchor is Church Street Station, although the closure of several of its restaurants and shows has lessened the appeal of the complex, which now centers mainly on the country-and-western Cheyenne Saloon. Despite this slowdown, the bar strip on the eastern side of Church Street near Orange Avenue remains very popular. On weekend evenings, the street is blocked to traffic, which makes it easy to zigzag between watering holes such as the Ybor Martini Bar and Mulvaney's, although hipper bars are found around the corner on Orange Avenue *(see p116).* *Church St bet. Orange Ave & I-4 • Map P3*

Lake Eola Fountain, Lake Eola Park

Church Street

Colonial Lanes
10 For more than 50 years, the venerable Colonial Lanes has offered patrons the sociable and quintessential blue-collar pastime of bowling. This 32-lane facility is a friendly and noisy place to knock over a few pins, so rent some shoes, pick out a ball, and let the computer keep score – but bear in mind that league bowling takes over the place between 6pm and 9pm every night, so

Bowling balls, Colonial Lanes

avoid those times, unless you're happy to watch. After the game, the place to go is the Colonial Lanes Bar & Restaurant, parts of which resemble a giant sunken living room (with bartenders standing on a lower floor than customers). Drinks are cheap, and the concept of rounding off prices never caught on here, so don't be surprised if your tab is a quirky $4.38. ◎ 400 N. Primrose Dr • Map P4 • 407-894-0361 • 9am–11:30pm daily • Free, but pay to play

A Day Downtown

Morning

Begin with a big healthy breakfast at JP's Everyday Gourmet (63 E. Pine St) before visiting the **Orange County Regional History Center**, a homespun place that reveals the pre-Disney history of the region. For lunch, wander over to the trendy **Baraka Café** (see p118). This fabulous bistro serves generous portions, so a grilled vegetable sandwich or chicken pasta salad should hit the spot.

Afternoon

After lunch, jump in the car or grab a cab to Loch Haven Park, where the **Orlando Museum of Art**, the **Orlando Science Center**, and the **Mennello Museum of American Folk Art** (for all see p113) reside within easy walking distance of each other. The Science Center, with its four floors of interactive fun, is the best bet for kids. Art lovers can easily hit the Mennello and the OMA in the same afternoon but if time is short, the OMA deserves priority. Make a dinner stop in the Vietnamese district where Vinh's Restaurant (1231 E. Colonial Dr) serves up a top-notch bowl of comforting *pho*, a traditional, and delicious noodle soup.

Evening

The downtown club scene starts late, so kick off with an early cocktail at **The Bösendorfer Lounge** (see p116). Fans of live music should head to **The Social** (see p116), where shows start around 10pm. Die-hard clubbers should try **The Club** (see p116), where the DJs play well into the early hours.

Left **Barbarella** Right **Tabu**

Nightspots

1 The Social
Orlando's best club for live music, bar none. The stage hosts an incredible variety of performers, from jazz to electronica. ✆ *54 N. Orange Ave • Map P3*

2 Tabu
This cavernous former theater is a dark and trendy magnet, largely for 20-somethings on the prowl. The music favors house and breakbeat. ✆ *46 N. Orange Ave • Map P3 • Closed Mon*

3 8 Seconds
A gigantic country and western hot spot that can hold a few thousand hardcore line dancers. There are also live bull-riding contests and truck races. ✆ *100 W. Livingston St • Map P3 • Closed Sun–Thu*

4 The Bösendorfer Lounge
With upscale elegance, this lounge is a rare place, perfect for sipping cocktails in stylish surroundings. Lounge singers and pianists play around the $250,000 Bösendorfer piano (Tue–Sat). ✆ *Westin Grand Bohemian Hotel, 325 S. Orange Ave • Map P3*

5 Cairo
Everything from house to retro-progressive is played at this multi-floored, Egyptian-themed club. There's also a rooftop reggae lounge. ✆ *22 S. Magnolia Ave • Map P3 • Closed Mon & Tue, & Thu*

6 Knock Knock
The DJs at this club-bar up the vibe without blowing anyone's eardrums. The perfect place to chill between clubs. ✆ *50 E. Central Blvd • Map P3 • Closed Mon*

7 Church Street
A two-block strip of bars, restaurants, and clubs that draws party people wanting to steer clear of the trendiness of other downtown clubs. ✆ *Church St, bet Orange Ave & I-4 • Map P3*

8 Bodhisattva Social Club
Tucked into a small brownstone, Bodhisattva has an intimate bar on ground level, while upstairs hosts live music (from folk to electronic bands) and DJs playing ambient tunes. The hipsters' bar of choice. ✆ *23 S. Court Ave • Map P3*

9 Icon
Step inside Orlando's home of house music, which offers a scrap metal decor, scantily dressed cage dancers, and a trendy crowd. ✆ *20 E. Central Blvd • Map P3 • Closed Sun & Mon, Wed & Thu*

10 Barbarella
This club-cum-music-venue has high-energy house in the front room and hard rock local bands on the outdoor stage. A small room features Goth sounds. ✆ *70 N. Orange Ave • Map P3 • Closed Sun–Tue*

Unless indicated Downtown's nightspots are open seven nights a week.

Price Categories

For a three-course	$	under $20
meal for one with half	$$	$20–$30
a bottle of wine (or	$$$	$30–$45
equivalent meal), taxes,	$$$$	$45–$60
and extra charges.	$$$$$	over $60

Sushi Hatsu

TOP 10 Restaurants & Cafés

1 Café Allegre
Downtown's best dining experience mixes bistro warmth with an adventurous menu of Asian, French, and Italian influences. ◈ 2401 Edgewater Dr • Map M2 • 407-872-2332 • Closed Sun & Mon • $$$$$

2 The Boheme
This outstanding old-world restaurant, with its sensual paintings and dark woods, serves game, steaks, and seafood to an upscale clientele. ◈ 325 S. Orange Ave • Map P3 • 407-581-4700 • $$$$$

3 Manuel's on the 28th
Guests at this upscale eatery rave about the international menu, which includes Atlantic sea scallops with crushed macadamia nuts, and the superb views. ◈ 390 N. Orange Ave • Map P3 • 407-246-6580 • Closed Sun & Mon • $$$$$

4 Baraka Café
Head here for a bistro ambience and hearty American food with a hint of Haitian flavoring, such as rum and honey-glazed port with mango salsa. ◈ 39 N. Orange Ave • Map P3 • 407-839-8500 • Closed Sun • $$$

5 Concha Me Crazy
This eatery serves souped-up traditional Caribbean dishes such as jerk shrimp, curry chicken, and conch chowder. ◈ 191 E. Pine St • Map P3 • 407-246-0011 • $$$$

6 Dexter's of Thornton Park
A favorite after-work spot, Dexter's offers exotic sandwiches, hearty salads, and entrees such as seared tuna and steak. ◈ 808 E. Washington St • Map P3 • 407-648-2777 • $$$

7 Sushi Hatsu
Central Florida's freshest and best sushi and sashimi come from this tiny, family-run operation. Cooked Japanese dishes are also available. ◈ 24 E. Washington St • Map P3 • 407-422-1551 • $$$

8 Little Saigon
This place stands out in the city's thriving Vietnamese area for its huge bowls of *pho*, fragrant soup brimming with meat, seafood, noodles, and spices. ◈ 1106 E. Colonial Dr • Map N3 • 407-423-8539 • $

9 White Wolf Café
This café serves great salads and Middle-Eastern-inspired fare in a former antiques store. It also sells most of its vintage furnishings. ◈ 1829 N. Orange Ave • Map N3 • 407-895-5590 • $

10 Deli Planet
Nothing beats this weird little sandwich shop, with its outer-space theme and awesome sandwiches, such as the Battlestar Garlica. Eat in or take away. ◈ 2315 S. Orange Ave • Map Q3 • 407-420-9152 • $

Unless stated, all restaurants advise reservations, take credit cards, and have DA, smoking tables, kids' menus, A/C, and vegetarian dishes.

Left **Winter Park street scene** Right **Cornell Fine Arts Museum**

Winter Park, Maitland, & Eatonville

TRUE TO ITS NAME, *Winter Park was chartered in 1887 as a winter resort for wealthy – and cold – Northerners. It evolved into a suburb of metropolitan Orlando, but still retains the charm and character of a wealthy, small town, with excellent shops, bars, and restaurants, and a sprinkling of interesting museums. The areas of Maitland and Eatonville, to the north and east, are more residential, but also have some worthwhile attractions, which make a pleasant change from south Orlando's mass-market theme parks.*

Winter Park Scenic Boat Tour

🔟 Sights & Attractions

1. Park Avenue
2. Charles Hosmer Morse Museum of American Art
3. Cornell Fine Arts Museum
4. Winter Park Scenic Boat Tour
5. Albin Polasek Museum & Sculpture Gardens
6. Waterhouse Residence & Carpentry Museum
7. Birds of Prey Center
8. Zora Neale Hurston National Museum of Fine Arts
9. Winter Park Farmers' Market
10. Enzian Theater

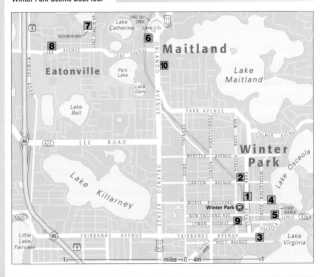

Park Avenue

1 The stretch of Park Avenue between Fairbanks and Swoope avenues is a thriving and delectable slice of urban living. This is the kind of manageable, old-style downtown, which is usually erased in the rush to suburbanize the Sunshine State. There's bucolic Central Park; buildings are rarely over three stories and contain fashionable shops or eateries at ground level; and all around, the sidewalks are full of people enjoying the day. ⓢ *Map L4*

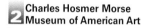

Park Avenue

range of European and American art – from the Renaissance to 20th century – is impeccably presented and of an unusually high quality for a small college art museum. ⓢ *100 Holt Ave • Map L4 • 407-646-2526 • Open 10am–5pm Tue–Fri, 1–5pm Sat & Sun • Free*

Charles Hosmer Morse Museum of American Art

2 The imposing, windowless walls of this museum rather ironically contain an outstanding collection of beautiful glass windows and objects by the American artist, Louis Comfort Tiffany. Other highlights include American ceramics and representative collections of late-19th- and early-20th-century paintings, graphics, and decorative arts. ⓢ *445 N. Park Ave • Map L4 • 407-645-5311 • Open 9:30am–4pm Tue–Sat (to 8pm Fri Sep–May), 1–4pm Sun • Adm*

Albin Polasek Museum & Sculpture Gardens

Winter Park Scenic Boat Tour

4 The wealthiest sections of Winter Park were built by a series of lakes and along small, winding canals. This boat tour has been running since 1938, and is part nature trip and part local history lesson. It cruises lazily past Winter Park landmarks and lakeside mansions encountering wildlife, while the skipper tells stories about the area's legendary society crowd. ⓢ *Morse Blvd at Lake Osceola • Map L4 • 407-644-4056 • Tours depart on the hour 10am–4pm daily • Adm*

Cornell Fine Arts Museum

3 The art collection at this museum, located on the scenic Rollins College Campus, is one of the oldest in the state. The

Charles Hosmer Morse Museum of American Art

Albin Polasek Museum & Sculpture Gardens

5 Sculptor Albin Polasek moved here to retire, but in fact he kept producing his figurative works until his death in 1965. Now listed on the National Register of Historic Places, the museum and its sculpture gardens contain works spanning Polasek's entire career. ⓢ *633 Osceola Ave • Map L4 • 407-647-6294 • Open 10am–4pm Tue–Sat, 1–4pm Sun • Adm*

Waterhouse Residence & Carpentry Museum

6 Historic Waterhouse Residence & Carpentry Museum

William H. Waterhouse was a carpenter who came to Central Florida in the early 1880s and built this lovely home overlooking Lake Lily. Pristinely restored and maintained by the Maitland Historical Society, the home, Waterhouse's carpentry shop, and the property's remarkable collection of handcrafted furniture offer a glimpse into the DIY days of Maitland's past. Woodworking buffs will be wowed by Waterhouse's extensive use of heart of pine, a wood rarely seen today. Tours lasting about 40 minutes are offered. The Waterhouse facilities nicely complement the Maitland Historical Museum and the Telephone Museum (see p61), both located just a few blocks away and also run by the Maitland Historical Society.
Ⓢ 820 Lake Lilly Dr • Map K3 • 407-644-2451• Open Thu–Sun noon–4.00pm • Adm

7 Audubon National Center for Birds of Prey

Think of this place as a halfway house for some of the most impressive examples of Florida's birdlife. It was created by the Florida Audubon Society to rescue,

Birds of Prey Center

rehabilitate, and release wounded raptors (birds of prey). Those that wouldn't survive being released into the wild are kept here, living a pampered existence in a lovely lakeside location, while helping to educate visitors about wildlife issues and conservation. Guests aren't allowed to observe the rehabilitation process, but permanent residents on view usually include vultures, bald eagles, screech owls, hawks, ospreys, and more. Ⓢ 1101 Audubon Way • Map K3 • 407 644-0190 • Open 10am–4pm Tue–Sun • Adm

8 Zora Neale Hurston National Museum of Fine Arts

Zora Neale Hurston earned fame as one of the brightest stars of Harlem's literary heyday in the 1920 and 1930s. Many of her most famous writings (including the 1937 novel, *Their Eyes Were Watching God*) reflected life in her hometown of Eatonville, the first incorporated African-American municipality in the USA. The front porches and stores of Eatonville, where Zora's characters lived and spun their tales, have long since disappeared, but she is not forgotten. This museum keeps the writer's memory alive, offering maps for a self-guided walking tour to the remaining literary landmarks of her neighbourhood. The museum also has rotating exhibits of work by contemporary African-American artists.
Ⓢ 227 E. Kennedy Blvd
• Map K3 • 407-647-3307
• Open 9am–4pm Mon– Fri
• Free

Winter Park Farmers' Market

9

Some farmers' markets are serious business, packed with old trucks and farmers selling mountains of vegetables just pulled from the earth. The Winter Park Farmers' Market is altogether a different affair. More of a social gathering on the village green, Winter Park's yuppies come here to mingle, buy potted flowers, preserves, and herbs, and indulge in fresh croissants, muffins, and breads. Yes, the required stacks of vegetables are here, too, but this is more of a coffee and brunch gathering. ✪ *721 W. England Ave • Map L4 • Open 7am–1pm Sat • Free*

Exhibit, Zora Neale Hurston National Museum of Fine Arts

Enzian Theater

10

The art of film tastes different at the Enzian. This not-for-profit 250-seat theater doesn't just show terrific American independent and foreign films, it also offers a full menu with beer, wine, and table service. Relax with dinner or snacks and enjoy films with all the comforts of sitting in your own living room (if that living room has a 33-ft (10-m) wide screen). As well as the regular schedule, the Enzian produces the 10-day Florida Film Festival *(see p64)* and smaller, niche festivals throughout the year. ✪ *1300 S. Orlando Ave • Map K3 • 407-629-1088 • Open evenings daily & weekend afternoons • Adm*

A Day in Winter Park

Morning

🕘 Begin with a hearty breakfast at the **Briarpatch Restaurant** *(see p123)*. You'll probably have to wait a bit, especially on weekends, so grab a newspaper. Then take time to wander the north end of **Park Avenue** *(see p119)*, where a multitude of charming one-off boutiques cater to upscale shopping tastes. At Cole Avenue pop in to the **Charles Hosmer Morse Museum** *(see p119)*; its outstanding collection of Tiffany glass is a must-see. Follow this with a relaxing trip on the **Winter Park Scenic Boat Tour** *(see p119)*, which departs from a dock on Morse Street, just a 15-minute walk away. On your return, lunch options are plentiful, but if the weather is good, grab one of the sidewalk tables at the **Village Bistro** *(see p122)* for some good food and serious people-watching.

Afternoon

After lunch, continue south on Park Avenue to Rollins College, home of the excellent **Cornell Fine Arts Museum** *(see p119)* and spend the rest of the afternoon enjoying this small but excellent collection.

Evening

Then, it's a ten-minute car ride north to Maitland's **Enzian Theater** where you can settle in to enjoy the latest in US and foreign independent films with a bottle of wine and a cheese plate. End the day at the bustling **Brio Tuscan Grille** *(see p123)* just a few minutes south by car, savoring a pink cosmopolitan or a gorgonzola-encrusted steak.

Left **Houston's** Right **Fiddler's Green**

TOP 10 Bars & Nightspots

1 Brio Tuscan Grille
The trendy grill at Brio is wildly popular, but a lot of people come just to hang out at the bar here. Cocktails flow fast and furious for a crowd of well-heeled locals. *See p123.*

2 Dexter's of Winter Park
Home to a serious collection of wines, this branch of Dexter's is more upscale than Down-town's, except on Thursdays when there's a band playing classic rock. ⊛ *558 W. New England Ave • Smoke-free • Map L4*

3 Fiddler's Green
An energetic Irish pub with darts, music, and a full selection of draft beers and stouts. Fiddler's stays open until 2am most nights, making it popular for a last round. The food is good, too. ⊛ *544 W. Fairbanks Ave • Map L4*

4 Park Plaza Gardens
With tables spilling out onto Park Avenue, this café bar is the bar of choice for an older set, who enjoy a cigar and glass of wine. *See p125.*

5 Shafer's Caffeehaus
The intimate upstairs room at this little nook often has live jazz. A nouveau German menu and a range of wines by the glass make this a popular stop. ⊛ *535 W. New England Ave • Map L4*

6 Copper Rocket Pub
With a small stage that hosts jazz jams to psycho rock, Copper Rocket is the only true music bar in the area. Microbrews and import beers fuel the young audience. ⊛ *106 Lake Ave • Map K3*

7 Blackfin Seafood Grill & Bar
The bar at this eaterie is often packed with an upscale crowd more interested in the score with each other than that of the sports matches on TV. Live jazz-funk groups play out back. ⊛ *460 N. Orlando Ave • Map L3*

8 Houston's
One of Winter Park's top spots in which to be seen. Maybe the draw is the generous glasses of wine poured here, or the fact that the entire restaurant menu is available at the bar. *See p123.*

9 An Tobar
An Irish bar in a hotel usually inspires yawns, but the authentic An Tobar gets thumbs up. The beer selection could be better, but the Guinness and Bass suit the low-key crowd. ⊛ *600 N. Lake Destiny Dr • Map K3*

10 Village Bistro of Winter Park
With cramped tables, brick walls, and a piano player singing show tunes, you might think you're in NYC's West Village. ⊛ *326 S. Park Ave • Map L4*

Winter Park's nightspots are usually open seven days a week.

Price Categories

For a three course meal for one with half a bottle of wine (or equivalent meal), taxes and extra charges.	
$	under $20
$$	$20–$30
$$$	$30–$45
$$$$	$45–$60
$$$$$	over $60

Brio Tuscan Grille

🔟 Cafés & Restaurants

1 Maison & Jardin
This seriously upscale place wins kudos and a loyal following for elegant service, a breathtaking wine list, and classic European fare. ❀ 430 Wymore Rd • Map K2 • 407-862-4410 • $$$$$

2 Trastevere Ristorante
The courtyard location and eclectic interior wins Trastevere praise as a romantic dinner spot. The Italian menu has an exquisite array of traditional dishes. ❀ 400 S. Orlando Ave • Map L3 • 407-628-1277 • No kids' menu • $$$$

3 Park Plaza Gardens
The menu at this garden restaurant is regional Americana, with a particular focus on seafood, such as blue crab cakes with mustard sauce. ❀ 319 S. Park Ave • Map L4 • 407-645-2475 • $$$$$

4 Winnie's Oriental Garden
Good Chinese food is rare in these parts. Winnie's, with its inventive menu, is a find. Try the Peking duck, or the salt and pepper shrimp. ❀ 1346 N. Orange Ave • Map L3 • 407 629-2111 • No kids' menu • $$$

5 Bubbalou's Bodacious BBQ
Smoked meat is the name of the game at this family joint. The sauces to put on range from mild to killer hot. ❀ 1471 Lee Rd • Map K3 • 407-628-1212 • No vegetarian dishes • No DA • $

6 Briarpatch Restaurant
Winter Park's homey breakfast landmark is known for big omelets and fresh fruit platters, but the creative, healthy American menu will make you consider returning for lunch or dinner. ❀ 252 N. Park Ave • Map L4 • 407-628-8651 • $$

7 Houston's
Here, various cuts of meat are chopped thick and cooked on a wood-burning grill. Portions are huge, particularly the salads and desserts. There are also seafood options. ❀ 215 S. Orlando Ave • Map L3 • 407-740-4005 • $$$

8 Brio Tuscan Grille
This local favorite has a huge dining room that buzzes with chatter and the sizzle of grilling in the open kitchen. ❀ 480 N. Orlando Ave • Map L3 • 407-622-5611 • $$$$

9 Thai Place
This place serves the best tom kha gai (spicy chicken soup with coconut milk) and pad thai (rice noodles with chicken, shrimp, and peanuts) in North Orlando. ❀ 501 N. Orlando Ave • Map L3 • 407-644-8449 • No kids' menu • $$$

10 Café de France
Despite the name, this eaterie has an international menu served in an upbeat setting. ❀ 526 S. Park Ave • Map L4 • 407-647-1869 • No kids' menu • No vegetarian dishes • $$$$$

 Unless stated, all restaurants advise reservations, take credit cards, and have DA, smoking tables, kids' menus, A/C, and vegetarian dishes.

STREETSMART

ORLANDO'S TOP 10

Left **Monorail, Orlando International Airport** Right **Summer theme park crowds**

🔟 Things to Know Before You Go

1 Orlando International Airport

Serving more than 100 cities worldwide, and handling 31 million passengers a year, this is the city's busiest airport. Forty scheduled airlines use it: the major domestic carriers include Delta, American, Northwest, US Airways, America West, and Southwest. British Airways, Virgin Atlantic, Air Canada, Iberia, and Saudi Arabian Airlines are some of its international carriers. Check the website (see p130) for information and maps to make sure you don't spend more time there than you need to. The airport is located about a 30-minute drive from Walt Disney World – if traffic is good.

2 Orlando Sanford International

Orlando's second airport, used primarily by international flights, is around an hour's drive from the Disney resorts. It is far smaller (used by just 1.2 million passengers per year) and promises a less crowded, less hectic start to a vacation.

3 Orlando Executive Airport

Situated just three miles (5 km) from the city's business center, Orlando's original airport is today used by private charters for both business and pleasure travelers.

4 US Entry Requirements for Canadian Visitors

Canadians only need some kind of photo ID and proof of residence to travel to the US.

5 US Entry Requirements for Overseas Visitors

Citizens from the UK, South Africa, Australia, New Zealand and many European countries may visit for up to 90 days without a visa if they have a valid passport. Other nationals should apply for a visa from their local US consulate or embassy well before they travel. For the latest information check on-line (www.state.gov).

6 Arriving by Train & Bus

Two Greyhound bus terminals and four Amtrak rail stations (including Sanford's Auto train terminal) serve the Orlando area. Tickets are rarely much cheaper than those for equivalent journeys by air.

7 Consolidators & Packagers

Consolidators buy bulk airline seats (and occasionally rooms) to sell at cheaper prices. Try 1-800-FLY-CHEAP (1-800-359-2432; www.1800flycheap.com). Packagers sell full or partial packages that can include flight, room, rental car, and theme park tickets. Some parks have their own; or try www.vactionpackager.com.

🕲 Disney packages • 407-828-8101 • www.disneyworld.com 🕲 SeaWorld packages • 1-800-423-8368 • www.seaworld.com 🕲 Universal packages • 407-224-7000 • www.universalorlando.com

8 Beat the Crowds

Theme park crowds are thinnest from the second week in September to the third week in November, the first two weeks of December, mid-January to mid-March, and late April through the third week of May. These are the periods when most American children are in school, although weekends are always busy.

9 Weather Wise

Heat and humidity can be oppressive in summer, when temperatures easily hit 90°F (32°C). Lightning is another summer threat. Get or stay inside if it approaches. High pollen counts in spring can make life miserable for allergy sufferers.

10 Online Planning

USA Tourist (www.usatourist.com) is one of the best multilingual resources. It has information on attractions, hotels, restaurants, and more in English, Spanish, French, Japanese, and German. Search engines are also useful for planning a trip, while MapQuest (www.mapquest.com) can help you plan a route once you've arrived.

Left **I-Ride Trolly** Center **Lynx Bus Stop** Right **Taxi**

🔟 Tips on Getting Around Orlando

1 Renting a Car

Most major car rental companies have offices at or near both major airports, as well as in town. Many also have shuttles serving the Amtrak and Greyhound stations. Most agencies offer special deals via their websites *(see p130)* or packagers. Local maps are provided, and staff can help plan the route to your hotel.

2 Navigating Orlando

The city's major north–south artery is Interstate Highway 4 (Hwy I-4), which connects the main tourist areas. The Bee Line Expressway (Hwy 528) is an east–west tollway useful for reaching the Kennedy Space Center *(see pp38–41)*. Most main roads suffer gridlock during rush hour (7–9am and 4–6pm daily).

3 Shuttle Options

Mears shuttle buses travel from Orlando International Airport to hotels (round trip $25 per adult to/from Disney World), and around the tourist areas, including the Kennedy Space Center. Quick Transportation charges $118 for up to six people for the same service, but offers personalized pickup and takes you straight to your destination. ✆ *Mears • 407-423-5566 • www.mearstransportation.com* ✆ *Quick Transportation • 407-354-2456 • www.quicktransportation.com*

4 Hotel Shuttles

Some hotels offer an airport shuttle service, and many offer transport to and from theme parks and other attractions several times per day. The service is usually free of charge to the parks nearest them, or available for a small charge to get to the others. Inquire about services when booking or planning your vacation.

5 Taking a Taxi

Taxis can be an economical way to get around for groups of four or five people. The fares from Orlando International and Orlando Sanford International airports to Walt Disney World are around $34 and $69 (plus tip) respectively. Extra charges apply at nights, weekends, and on public holidays. Cabs are easily found at airports and major hotels – otherwise call *(see p131)*, as they are not that easy to flag down in the street.

6 The Disney Transportation System

Disney's free transportation system (monorail, buses, water taxis, and ferries) means you can save money by not renting a car and paying for gas and parking. It's best for guests who will spend most of their time with Mickey. But the circuits are set in stone and it can sometimes take an hour to reach some destinations in the resort.

7 The I-Ride Trolley

This service is a convenient and cheap way to get from A to B along the Universal, Sea-World, and International Drive corridor. Trolleys run every 15 minutes, 7am–11:30pm daily, and make 54 stops. Exact change is required. ✆ *407-354-5656 • www.iridetrolley.com*

8 Lynx Buses

Other than walking or cycling, Orlando's public bus system is the least popular way for most visitors to get around: buses can be frustratingly slow. Bus stops are marked with a paw print. Exact change is required. ✆ *Lynx Downtown Bus Terminal • 78 W Central Blvd • 407-841-2279 • www.golynx.com*

9 Hiring a Limo

The least economical but most luxurious way to get around is by limousine – an option for travelers who want to be pampered and who have deeper pockets. ✆ *Advantage Limousine Service • 407-438-8888 • www.advantagelimo.com*

10 Walking

This is one of the USA's most dangerous cities for pedestrians: apart from wide highways with fast-moving traffic, there's a shortage of sidewalks, crosswalks, and street lights.

Left **Newspaper vending machines** Right **Kissimmee Convention & Visitors Bureau**

🔟 Sources of Information

1 Orlando/Orange Co. Convention & Visitors Bureau

Billed as "the official destination marketing organization for Orlando", this group provides an impressively comprehensive service. Their website is outstanding, offering up-to-date information and on-line booking, while the office can provide maps, directions, and answer questions. ✆ *8723 International Dr • 407-363-5872 • www.orlandoinfo.com*

2 Kissimmee/St. Cloud Convention & Visitors Bureau

Focusing on the south of Orlando, this organization offers an excellent website and an office stocked with hundreds of brochures from area attractions. ✆ *1925 E. Irlo Bronson Hwy. • 407-847-5000 • www.floridakiss.com*

3 Orlando Sentinel

The sole major daily newspaper in town is notoriously conservative in political matters, but the Friday edition carries an excellent arts and events section called the Calendar. There's an online version too (www.orlandosentinel.com).

4 Orlando Weekly

O-Town's primary "alternative" paper is this free weekly, which carries excellent and extremely detailed club and arts listings. The columnists – all good, some hilarious – know the local scene intimately. The paper's website (www.orlandoweekly.com) offers all the articles as well as terrific search capabilities for movie and music listings. The paper is available in restaurants, shops, clubs, convenience stores, and street boxes all over town.

5 Watermark

This free bi-weekly newspaper is the voice of Orlando's extensive gay and lesbian community. Not particularly radical, it offers splendid coverage of arts and events and is the best resource for clubs, shows, and more for the community. Available at gay-friendly businesses and in street boxes. There's also an on-line version: www.watermarkonline.com.

6 Gay, Lesbian, & Bisexual Community Services of Central Florida

This "lesbigay" community center is the city's clearinghouse for gay community information, ranging from art openings to health alerts. The organization regularly sponsors a variety of cultural events around town. ✆ *407-228-8272 • www.glbcc.org*

7 News Channel 13

This is Orlando's own version of CNN – a 24-hour cable news channel devoted to O-Town. It is probably most useful to visitors for the weather update that runs every ten minutes (1:01, 1:11, 1:21, etc). ✆ *Only available on TVs subscribed to Time Warner Cable*

8 WTKS 104.1-FM

As well as national media superstar and controversial presenter Howard Stern's syndicated show (weekday mornings), the schedule of this radio station is filled with local talk radio personalities. All offer an interesting window into Orlando's current state of mind.

9 WMFE 90.7-FM

The area's best public radio station is best known for intelligent hourly news. The rest of the day offers light classical music – useful for calming down frustrated drivers in I-4 road jams *(see p140)* – with weekends turned over to syndicated public radio shows.

10 Brochure Racks

Virtually every hotel, restaurant, and attraction offers a huge lobby display packed with brochures and tourist guides covering almost all the hotels, restaurants, and smaller attractions in the area. Besides the maps and general information, discount coupons are common in these publications, so they're worth picking up *(see p133)*.

Camp SeaWorld

TOP 10 Behind-the-Scenes Tours

1 Backstage Magic
Disney's most complete but expensive tour is ideal for guests who have to know what makes things tick. The seven-hour visit explores the inner workings of Epcot technology, the art of animation at Disney-MGM Studios, and the Magic Kingdom's underground operations hub. ✆ 407-939-8687 • Max 20 people, 16 yrs & over • 9am Mon–Fri

2 Keys to the Kingdom
A useful, four-to-five hour Magic Kingdom taster tour for guests who'd like to see what's on offer before they really get started. It gives a basic park orientation as well as a glimpse of some of the usually hidden high-tech magic. ✆ 407-939-8687 • Min age 16 yrs • Cost does not include park adm • 8:30am, 9:30am, 10am, & 1:30pm daily

3 Hidden Treasures of World Showcase
This three-hour tour offers a closer view than most park guests get of Epcot's multi-cultural treasures. ✆ 407-939-8687 • Max 20 people, min age 16 yrs • Cost does not include park adm • 9am Tue & Thu

4 Family Magic Tour
Kids love this two-hour scavenger hunt in Disney World's most child-friendly park, the Magic Kingdom. Characters also meet guests at the end of the tour. ✆ 407-939-8687 • Cost does not include park adm • 9:30 & 11:30am daily

5 VIP Tours
Both Disney and Universal offer VIP tours – at a price. Disney's lets guests create their own itinerary, which could take in one or more parks, meals, golf, spa treatments, and more. The tour includes reserved show seating but not front-of-the-line access to rides. ✆ Disney • 407-560-4033 • Up to 10 people per tour, 5-hour min ✆ Universal • 407-363-8295 • 10am & noon daily

6 Gardens of the World
A fascinating three-hour tour through some of the finest landscaping in the theme-park world, as Disney horticulturists describe the gardens and growing techniques used at Epcot. ✆ 407-824-4321 • Min age 16 yrs • Cost does not include park adm • 9:30am Tue & Thu

7 Yuletide Fantasy
It's hard to beat Disney's Christmas celebration. This three-hour tour gives guests a front-row look at how the four theme parks and Fort Wilderness Lodge resort are transformed into a winter wonderland. Highlights include a candlelight procession and Epcot's massed choir. This tour is guaranteed to get visitors into the holiday spirit. ✆ 407-824-4321 • Park adm not required • 9am Mon–Sat Nov 30–Dec 24

8 Camp SeaWorld
During the summer, SeaWorld offers several day programs to suit all budgets. The camps are divided by age from pre-school through 8th grade (13 yrs) and are designed to help kids better understand the marine animal world. There are family sleep-over programs, too. ✆ 407-370-1380 • Jun–Aug

9 To the Rescue
This is an hour-long tour of SeaWorld's rescue and rehabilitation efforts (see p31). The tour goes through critical-care and quarantine areas, as well as laboratories and surgical units. ✆ 407-351-3600 • Cost does not include park adm • Times vary

10 Polar Expedition Guided Tour
SeaWorld's cold-climate creatures, including beluga whales and the polar bears Klondike and Snow, are the stars of this hour-long tour. It finishes at the avian research facility where guests get to meet and touch a penguin. ✆ 407-351-3600 • Cost does not include park adm • Times vary

Tours should be reserved at least one month in advance.

Useful Addresses

Tourist Information

Central Florida Tourist Information Center
4834 W. Irlo Bronson Memorial Hwy (K) • 1-800-396-1883

Tourist Information Center
5825 International Dr (I-D) • 407-363-2901

Websites

Citysearch
orlando.citysearch.com

Digital City
www.digitalcity.com/orlando

Go2Orlando
www.go2orlando.com

FLAUSA
www.flausa.com

Inside Central Florida
www.icflorida.com

Themeparks.com
www.themeparks.com

Airports

Orlando Executive Airport (ORL)
501 Herndon Ave • 407-894-9831 • www.orlando airports.net

Orlando International Airport (MCO)
1 Airport Blvd • 407-825-2001 • www.orlando airports.net

Orlando Sanford Airport (SFB)
2 Red Cleveland Blvd, Sanford • 407-585-4000 • www.osi-airport.com

American Automobile Association (AAA)

4300 E.Colonial Dr • 407-894-3333 • www.aaasouth.com

Amtrak Train Stations

1400 Sligh Blvd (DO) • 407-843-7611 • www.amtrak.com

150 W. Morse Blvd (WP) • 407-645-5055 • www.amtrak.com

600 Persimmon Ave (Sanford) • 407-323-9966 • www.amtrak.com

111 Dakin St (K) • 1-407-933-1170 • www.amtrak.com

Greyhound Bus Terminals

103 E. Dakin Ave (K) • 1-888-332-6363 • www.greyhound.com

555 N. John Young Pkwy (DO) • 1-888-332-6363 • www.grey hound.com

Car Rental

Alamo
8200 McCoy Rd • 1-800-327-9633 • www.alamo.com

Avis
8600 Hangar Blvd • 1-800-831-2847 • www.avis.com

Budget
8855 Rent A Car Rd • 1-800-527-7000 • www.budget.com

Dollar
8735 Rent A Car Rd • 1-800-800-4000 • www.dollar.com

Enterprise
7652 Narcoossee Rd • 1-800-325-8007 • www. enterprise.com

Hertz
5601 Butler National Dr • 1-800-654-3131 • www.hertz.com

National
8350 Hangar Blvd • 1-800-227-7368 • www.national car.com

Thrifty
5600 Butler National Dr • 1-800-847-4389 • www. thrifty.com

Banks

AmSouth Bank
111 N. Orange Ave (DO) • 1-800-267-6884

5401 S. Kirkman Rd (WDW) • 1-800-267-6884

Bank of America
390 N. Orange Ave (DO) • 1-800-299-2265

First Union
7204 Sand Lake Rd (I-D) • 1-800-275-3862

Huntington National Bank
7625 Sand Lake Rd (I-D) • 407-352-9363

SunTrust
3357 Vine St (K) • 1-800-786-8787

400 S. Park Ave (WP) • 1-800-786-8787

Washington Mutual
7674 Dr. Phillips Blvd (WDW) • 1-800-788-7000

Credit Cards

American Express
1-800-297-1234 • www. americanexpress.com

Diners Club
1-800-234-6377 • www. dinersclub.com

Discover
1-800-347-2683 • www. discovercard.com

MasterCard
1-800-62-277-7747 • www. mastercard.com

Key: *DO: Downtown; I-D: International Drive; K: Kissimmee; WDW: Walt Disney World & Lake Buena Vista; WP: Winter Park & Maitland*

Visa
1-800-847-2911 • www.
visa.com

Hospitals

Celebration Health
400 Celebration Pl (WDW)
• 407-303-4000

Florida Hospital
7727 Lake Underhill Rd
(DO) • 407-303-8110

200 Hilda St (K) • 407-846-
4343

Sand Lake Hospital
9400 Turkey Lake Rd (I-D)
• 407-351-8550

**Winter Park Memorial
Hospital**
200 N. Lakemont Ave (WP)
• 407-646-7000

Walk-In Clinics

**Centra Care Walk-In
Medical Care**
12139 S. Apopka Vineland
Rd (WDW) • 407-239-
7777

**Century Walk-In
Medical Center**
7801 W. Irlo Bronson
Memorial Hwy (K) • 407-
397-4900

ExpressCare
2700 Professional Pkwy
(DO) • 407-656-2055

**Orlando Regional Walk-
In Medical Care**
8324 International Dr (I-D)
• 407-351-3035

**University Walk-In
Medical Center**
2830 Casa Aloma Way (WP)
• 407-678-5554

24-hour Pharmacy

Eckerd Drugs
1205 W. Vine St (K) • 407-
847-5174

670 Lee Rd (WP) • 407-
628-4550

Walgreens
2420 E. Colonial Dr (DO)
• 407-894-5361

6201 International Dr
(I-D) • 407-345-8311

13502 Apopka Vineland Rd
(WDW) • 407-827-1000

Dentists

Advanced Dental Care
4020 S. Semoran Blvd (DO)
• 407-277-5787

Coast Dental
2200 E. Irlo Bronson Memorial Hwy (K) • 407-935-1772

2951 Vineland Rd (WDW)
• 407-396-1288

**Greenburg Dental
Associates**
4780 S. Kirkman Rd (I-D)
• 407-292-7373

7762 University Blvd (WP)
• 407-671-0001

Help Lines

Central Florida Helpline
407-740-7477

**Community Services
Network**
407-897-6464

Help Now of Osceola
407-847-3286

Internet Access

Kinko's Copies
9800 International Dr (I-D)
• 407-363-2831 • www.
kinkos.com

2145 Aloma Ave (WP)
• 407-677-9950 • www.
kinkos.com

The NetKaffee
22 Broadway St (K) • 407-
943-7500 • www.net
kaffee.com

Orlando Public Library
101 E. Central Blvd (DO)
• 407-835-7323

South Orange Library
11346 S. Orange Blossom Tr
(WDW) • 407-858-4779

Post Offices

46 E. Robinson St (DO)
• 1-800-275-8777

10450 Turkey Lake Rd (I-D)
• 1-800-275-8777

2600 Michigan Ave (K)
• 1-800-275-8777

12133 S. Apopka Vineland
Rd (WDW) • 407-238-0223

300 N. New York Ave (WP)
• 407-275-8777

Police

City of Kissimmee Police
8 N. Stewart Ave (K) • 407-
846-3333 • Emergency: 911

City of Orlando Police
100 S. Hughey Ave (I-D)
• 407-246-2414 • Emer-
gency: 911

Orange County Sherriff
2400 W. 33rd St (DO) • 407-
737-2400 • Emergency: 911

Osceola County Sheriff
400 Simpson Rd (K) • 407-
348-2222 • Emergency: 911

Winter Park Police
401 S. Park Ave (WP) • 407-
644-1313 • Emergency: 911

Consulates

Australia
2525 S.W. Third Ave, Ste 208,
Miami • (305) 857-0040

Canada
200 S. Biscayne Blvd, Ste
1600, Miami • (305) 579-
1600

Ireland
2511 N.E. 31st Court, Light-
house Point • (954) 785-3427

United Kingdom
200 S. Orange Ave, Ste 2110,
Orlando • 407-426-7855

For more on tourist information **See p128**

Left **Belz Designer Outlet Center** Center **Souvenirs from SeaWorld** Right **Beltz Factory Outlet Center**

🔟 Tips on Shopping & Tickets

1 Shopping Hours
Shops in theme parks keep the same hours as the parks. Malls and outlets are usually open from 9 or 10am until 9pm Monday to Saturday and at least noon to 6pm on Sunday. Shops outside the main tourist areas tend to open from 9am to 5pm Monday through Saturday.

2 Sales Tax
With the exception of groceries and some medications, all purchases in Orlando are subject to a 6 per cent state and local sales tax.

3 Sales
Look for winter-wear bargains from March through April, and summer bargains from August to October as the seasonal stock changes. In August, with the approach of the new school year, there are good buys on kids' clothes. The day after Thanksgiving is the biggest shopping day of the year, with huge pre-Christmas sales attracting hordes of shoppers.

4 Outlets
Outlet stores sell last season's fashions at discounted prices. Shoppers who know the suggested retail prices of the goods they seek will be able to tell what is – and what isn't – a bargain. Some stores promise as much as 75 per cent discount and some actually deliver.

Others don't. The big players here are the Orlando Premium and Belz outlets *(see p66)*.

5 Gifts & Souvenirs
Apart from cheap T-shirts, stuffed animals, and baseball caps, Orlando does have some more original souvenirs. These include Florida oranges, alligator meat and leather products, and manatee memorabilia.

6 Shipping Home
If you have bought more souvenirs than you can carry home, why not ship them? Disney and Universal parks, resorts, and shops can make the arrangements, usually via United Parcel Service (UPS). Do-it-yourselfers must take their packages to UPS (call 1-800-742-5877 for the nearest center) or the US Postal Service (1-800-275-8777).

7 Buy Theme Park Tickets Online
Disney (www.disneyworld.com) allows guests to buy tickets online, saving on time waiting in line, but they must be picked up in person. Universal (www.universalorlando.com) mails online tickets to buyers; buy at least five weeks in advance. SeaWorld's online service (www.seaworld.com) lets buyers print out their tickets and, when they arrive at the park, go straight to the turnstiles, where they are verified.

8 Multi-Day & Multi-Park Passes
Disney's Park Hopper and Park Hopper Plus tickets are valid for four to seven days. Both include unlimited entry to the four parks; the Park Hopper Plus tickets also include entry to other Disney attractions. The discounts aren't great, but you save time waiting in line. Universal (which also offers a separate two-to-three-day pass for Universal Parks only), SeaWorld, Wet 'n Wild, and Tampa's Busch Gardens have joined up to offer the unlimited access, 14-day FlexTicket.

9 Cutting in Line
Disney (FastPass) and Universal and SeaWorld (Express) offer a system that cuts out the long wait for the most popular rides and shows. Just slide your ticket through the turnstile to get an allocated time for your visit. When it's time, simply go to the particular attraction's designated entrance to take your place.

10 Concierge Desks
Most upscale and some moderately priced hotels have concierge desks in the lobby. They're great places to make restaurant reservations or buy tickets for theme parks and other attractions. They don't give discounts, but most do offer the convenience of waiting in a short line as opposed to a long one in the parks.

Left **Hotel shuttle bus** Right **Leaflets in a hotel lobby**

🔟 Tips for the Budget Conscious

1 The Magicard
The Orlando/Orange County CVB's *(see p128)* Magicard offers $500 worth of discounts on accommodation, car rentals, attractions, meals, shopping, and more. It also offers deals that combine rooms with attraction and theme park tickets. Each card is valid for up to six people, and it's free. Allow four weeks for delivery.
☏ 407-363-5872 • www.orlandoinfo.com

2 Hotel Handouts
Many hotels and motels offer freebies such as continental breakfasts, evening hors d'oeuvres, and newspapers. Their coupon racks are stuffed with two-for-one and other special deals on meals and attractions. For those without a car, most hotels have free or low-fee shuttle services to the parks.

3 Newspaper Coupons
The Sunday travel sections in many major US newspapers lure people to Orlando with offers of coupons, cheap fares, and package deals. Once here, read the Orlando Sentinel (especially Friday's Calendar section), as well as the free papers available on street corners and in hotel lobbies, all of which feature lots of discounts and offers. *See p128.*

4 Rooms with Cooking Facilities
Travelers can save big by booking a room with a kitchen, kitchenette, or even just a microwave and refrigerator. Apart from Walt Disney World properties, most accommodation is close to supermarkets or delicatessens, some of which deliver for a small fee.

5 Pack a Snack & Water
Theme-park prices for refreshments are 30–50 per cent higher than what people pay outside the parks. The parks prohibit coolers (containers for keeping food and drink cool), but guests can bring their own bottled water and snacks. Some parks have fountains, but the water in Central Florida does not taste particularly sweet.

6 Eat Big Early & Late
It's often unnecessary to eat three big meals a day, particularly in the hottest months of the year. If you want to skip, or go light on, lunch, you can eat well – and cheaply – before and after your theme-park visit by having a low-priced, all-you-can-eat, buffet breakfast and an early-bird dinner *(see p134)*.

7 Fast Food & Family Restaurants
Orlando is chock-full of fast-food outlets. The city also has an abundance of very well-priced family restaurants *(see pp70–71)*. Most have kids' menus, which can be even cheaper at lunchtime.

8 OTIX!
The cultural crowd isn't left out of the discount mix. The city's CVB *(see p128)* regularly has half-price tickets, including those for opera, ballet, music, and theater. The tickets are for same-day performances, and while information is available by phone, the tickets must be picked up in person. ☏ 407-872-2382

9 Staying at Disney on the Cheap
People who really want to stay at Disney World, but can't afford the prices, can find the cheapest rates at the All-Star resorts *(see p142)*. Rack rates (those anyone can get without a discount) are extraordinarily reasonable and kids also stay free. But be warned: rooms at these "value" resorts are very cramped.

10 Gas for Renters
Never buy gas for a rental car from the car hire company itself. Some of their offers sound enticing, especially those offering cheaper gas if you buy up front rather than when the car is returned. Most of the time, fuel prices are cheaper – sometimes much cheaper – around town.

Buffet breakfast

TOP 10 Tips on Eating & Drinking

1 Disney World's Priority Seating
Disney restaurants don't take reservations. In their place, they use what they call a priority seating system. Callers are given a time to arrive; when they turn up, the next available table is given to them (as opposed to a table being held open). Note that all restaurants inside Disney parks, except Animal Kingdom's Rainforest Café, require park admission.

2 Reservations
Whenever restaurants accept reservations, make them – especially in the main tourist areas of I-Drive, Lake Buena Vista, and along Irlo Bronson Memorial Highway in Kissimmee. Not having a reservation can mean waiting two hours for a table during prime dining time, usually 6–8:30pm. Some restaurants refuse to seat diners who have not reserved in advance and upscale eateries may be unable to accommodate you unless you reserve far ahead.

3 Gratuities
Wait staff expect a tip of at least 15 per cent. Those who are particularly helpful may deserve 20 per cent; you may want to give just 10 per cent to those who aren't. Some restaurants now add tips to the bill, so check before paying.

4 Smoking
Disney restaurants are all smoke-free. Due to the demand for toxin-free environments by diners, more and more Orlando eateries are following Disney's lead. For now, smoking tables are available in many restaurants. When making a reservation, specify if you want a smoking table or one well away from smokers.

5 Buffet Breakfast Bargains
There are several modestly priced, all-you-can-eat breakfast buffets around town (especially on I-Drive and in Kissimmee). For a handful of dollars, you can fill your stomach and save money by eating a light lunch or skipping it altogether.

6 Early Birds
Some value restaurants offer cut-rate meals when business is slow, which is usually 4–6pm Mon–Fri. These early-bird deals are usually advertised outside and are offered in the free coupon books found in hotel lobbies and tourist attractions. Many of these restaurants also offer 2-for-1 drink specials during these times.

7 Lunch Menus vs Dinner Menus
Many upscale restaurants are not only hard to get in to at dinnertime, but the menus are very expensive. The lunch menu might have fewer options, and portions tend to be a little less generous, but the prices are lower. To save money – and your digestive system – consider eating your main meal at mid-day and eating lighter at night.

8 Special Diets
Some restaurants that don't normally offer meat- and seafood-free options are happy to fix vegetarian dishes, with prior warning. Disney restaurants go one step further and provide for a variety of other needs, including kosher, fat- or sugar-free, plus lactose intolerance and allergies. Give 24 hours' notice. ✆ 407-824-2222 (407-939-3463 if staying on Disney property).

9 Happy Hours
Many bars (and restaurants) have happy hours, usually from 4–7pm, when drinks are often two for the price of one. They sometimes serve special hors d'oeuvres as well.

10 Hotel Mini Bars
Put bluntly, these are rip-offs. Years ago, inventive guests drank the good stuff and refilled the bottles with cheap brands. So now the mini bars have a sensor: remove the bottle for 10 seconds and you get charged – a lot – for it.

Left **Sun protection** Right **24-hour pharmacy**

TOP 10 Health Tips

1 Heat, Sun & Insects

Heat and humidity during the summer season (June to mid-September) can cause dehydration, so be sure to drink at least two quarts (two liters) of fluids (preferably water) each day, and wear a wide-brimmed hat and airy clothes. Not only does too much sun result in nasty burns, but it can also cause sun poisoning. Use a sunscreen with a high protection factor. And as much as Disney and Universal want to erase blood-sucking flies and mosquitoes, they can't, so remember to use insect repellent in summer.

2 911

This is the number to call for emergency health matters and for immediate police or fire assistance.

3 Hospitals & First Aid

Ask at your hotel or resort reception for the nearest hospital. Make sure you have some kind of insurance, otherwise hospital costs can be crippling. All of the major parks have first-aid clinics for minor ailments.

4 Ask-A-Nurse

This free telephone line is one of the most trusted referral services in Central Florida. Callers tell the nurse what the problem is, basic advice is given, and then they refer you to an appropriate doctor, dentist, hospital, or out-patient clinic. The service is free, but the treatment isn't. ✆ 407-870-1700

5 In-Room Medical Care

House calls are a thing of the past in most US cities, but the tourist areas in Orlando have two services that make house and hotel-room calls. Doctors on Call Service and Centra Care In-Room Services cover most of the areas from Downtown south to Disney and Kissimmee. ✆ Doctors on Call Service • 407-399-3627 ✆ Centra Care In-Room Services • 407-238-2000

6 Centra Care Walk-In Clinics

Centra Care (affiliated with the Florida Hospital) has walk-in clinics scattered throughout Orange, Seminole, and Osceola counties (see p131). These clinics can handle minor emergencies (broken limbs, cuts requiring stitches, and fevers), but not life-threatening situations, for which you should call 911.

7 24-Hour Pharmacies

Several drug stores sell over-the-counter and prescription drugs around the clock (see p131). Additional pharmacies, with regular hours, are listed in the Yellow Pages.

8 Dental Referral Service

This nationwide, toll-free service helps people to find the nearest suitable dentist. The telephones are answered 8am–8pm Monday–Friday; the automated answering service informs callers of the website then puts them on hold to speak to an operator. Those who prefer to choose for themselves, or anyone needing 24-hour aid, should use the Yellow Pages (or see p131). ✆ 1-888-343-3440 or 1-800-511-8663 • www.dentalreferral.com

9 Poison Control

This 24-hour hotline can and has saved lives. Operators can help deal with a problem, summon rescuers, and answer questions. But, don't overlook 911 for any emergency situation. ✆ 1-800-282-3171.

10 Florida Tourism Industry Marketing Corp

While it shouldn't be used for emergencies, this tourism-funded group can provide basic information about medical services and assistance throughout the state. It also has a range of other services, including assistance with lost credit cards and documents, help with accidents, directions, and more. Operators can help in more than 150 languages. ✆ 1-800-647-9284

Left **ATM machine** Right **Quarters (25¢) & pennies (1¢)**

🔟 Communications & Money Tips

1 Making Phone Calls

Orlando's explosive growth in recent years has created a numbers problem for telephone companies. Calling local numbers requires dialing a 10-digit number – the area code (Central Florida's is 407), plus the seven digit phone number. If calling a number with a different area (or toll-free) code, dial 1 before the code and telephone number.

2 Internet Access

Internet cafes (see p131) offer email and internet services for varying prices. Public libraries offer free access to the internet.

3 Languages

Disney, Universal, and larger hotels have multilingual staff who speak Spanish, French, German, and, in some cases, Dutch, Japanese, and other languages. They also have information printed in these languages. The Orlando/Orange County Convention & Visitors Bureau and USA Tourist have multilingual websites.
🔗 www.orlandoinfo.com
🔗 www.usatourist.com

4 Post Offices

The United States Postal Service (USPS) has five post offices in the Orlando area. Opening hours vary, but they are usually 9am to 5pm weekdays, although some open Saturday mornings as well. Drugstores and hotels often sell stamps, but they are slightly more expensive than those sold at post offices. Mailboxes, which are blue, are on most main streets and in hotels. Most major hotels also have daily collection services.

5 Credit Cards & Traveler's Checks

Most hotels, restaurants, attractions, and shops accept American Express, Diners Club, Discover, MasterCard, and Visa credit cards. Some also take Carte Blanche and JCB cards. US dollar denominations of American Express, Thomas Cook, and Visa traveler's checks are widely accepted with ID.

6 Currency & Exchanges

Dollar notes come in $1, $5, $10, $20, $50, and $100 bills. Coins in circulation are of 1 cent, 5 cents (a nickel), 10 cents (a dime), and 25 cents (a quarter) value. One-dollar and 50 cent coins exist but are very rare. Currency exchanges are based at all the airports, major branches of banks, and near guest services or guest relations in all major theme parks.

7 ATMs

Automatic Teller Machines (ATMs) are located at almost all bank branches, in all major theme parks, major shopping malls, some hotels, and at airports. Most also accept withdrawals on American Express, MasterCard, and Visa credit cards. There is a $1.50 to $3 advance charge for cards not affiliated to that particular bank. It's often cheaper to use a debit card, but not all debit systems are supported by US banks; check the symbols on the ATM to see if yours is one that is accepted.

8 Bank Opening Hours

Most Central Florida banks are open 9am to 4pm weekdays (to 6pm on Friday). A few branches also open Saturday mornings. Most have ATMs with 24-hour access.

9 Western Union

International money transfers can be sent to more than 101,000 Western Union agents and offices in 187 countries. They can also arrange international telegrams.
🔗 1-800-225-2274

10 Taxes

The USA doesn't have a national sales tax. Instead, individual states and counties set the rate of sales tax. Florida levies a six per cent state, or state and local tax, on everything except groceries and certain medicines. Hotels also add an extra three to five per cent bed tax (see p141).

Left **Valuables** Center **Orange County Sheriff's car** Right **Residential speed limit**

🔟 Safety Tips

1 On the Coast
Florida's beaches are usually well supervised by lifeguards, but still keep a close eye on young children and stick to areas where you can see the lifeguards. The same goes for rivers and pools.

2 Non-Emergency Numbers
Outside city limits, county sheriff's offices (see p131) are the primary police agencies: in Central Florida they are in Orange County, Osceola County, and Seminole County. For traffic and highway-related matters, call the Florida Highway Patrol. For coastal safety issues, contact the Florida Marine Patrol. ✆ *Florida Highway Patrol • 407-897-5959* ✆ *Florida Marine Patrol • 407-383-2740*

3 Hurricanes
The coast is usually hit hardest by hurricanes, but Central Florida is also affected. If caught in one, stay inside, away from windows, and have lots of water, canned food, and a flashlight to hand. For more tips and up-to-date forecasts, see the Hurricane Weather Center. ✆ *http://hurricane.weather center.com*

4 General Safety
Always keep car and hotel-room doors locked. Before driving, ask the rental-car company, your hotel's front-desk staff, or the Florida Tourism Industry Marketing Corporation (see p135) for the safest and most direct route to your destination. Don't let strangers change your currency, and when paying for anything, check you've been given the correct change before leaving the premises.

5 Valuables
Smart travelers leave valuables at home. If you do bring watches, jewelry, or other items of value, keep them in a hotel safe. The safes in hotel rooms should only be used for less valuable items. It's also advisable to carry credit cards or traveler's checks rather than large amounts of cash.

6 Stay in Populated, Well-Lit Areas
Orlando doesn't have the same crime rate as many cities, but it has its share of thieves who prey on the unsuspecting. At night, avoid badly lit areas (especially Downtown's westside, south of Colonial Drive), and at all times be wary of pickpockets.

7 Lost Children
Nothing frightens a parent or guardian more than turning away for a moment only to find their child gone. It happens every day in Orlando's theme parks. To help staff reunite families, children under seven should wear tags with their name, hotel, and a contact number on it. When any member of your group gets lost, find a park employee for assistance.

8 Seat Belts
Florida law requires seat belts to be worn by the driver and all passengers over the age of three. Children three years and under must ride in a car seat – most rental-car agencies can provide them. Those who don't heed the seat-belt law risk a fine of $50.

9 Drinking & Driving
In a word: Don't. In the best case, it can be costly. In the worst case, it can be deadly. Florida strictly enforces this law. Violators risk time in jail if convicted of a drink-driving offense. Have a designated driver in the group, skip alcohol for the night, use public transport, or grab taxis. Police are known to survey bars to see who is drinking, then wait outside until drinkers get in a car to drive off, when they are tested.

10 Speed Limits
Speed limits on interstates, toll roads, and major highways range from 55 to 70 mph (88–112 kmph). On smaller highways, the limit is 45 mph (72 kmph), and in residential areas, it's 30 to 35 mph (48–56 kmph). Fines begin at $160, doubling if it's in a school or construction zone.

Left **Mobility products** Center **Disabled parking facility** Right **Mature travelers**

Tips for Seniors & Disabled People

1 Mature Travelers Guide

The Orlando/Orange County CVB's Mature Travelers Guide offers nearly $300 worth of discount coupons for seniors. It also reviews places that may appeal to them. ✆ 407-363-5872 • www.orlandoinfo.com

2 AARP

The AARP (American Association of Retired Persons) is America's most vocal group for the elderly, but it doesn't forget there's room for fun. The website's travel articles are available to the public, but only members find out about AARP's travel deals and discounts. Membership costs are minimal. ✆ 1-202-434-2277 • www. aarp.org

3 Elderhostel

This educational travel organization sends people 55 and over on courses (usually for a week) all over the world. The choice of courses in Orlando is astounding, from travel photography to politics and philosophy. Stay at retreats, hotels, or campsites. ✆ 1-877-426-8056 • www.elderhostel.org

4 Disney Grandkids & You Getaway

Knowing that a lot of seniors come to Orlando with their grandkids, Disney occasionally offers discounted packages. Most include three nights in a Disney hotel, multiple-day tickets to the parks, and a range of goodies for the kids, such as dolls and autograph books. ✆ 407-934-7639 • www.disneyworld.com

5 Yvonne's Property Management

This service leases more than 20 wheelchair-accessible houses and villas in Davenport, a 15 minute drive southwest of Disney. They have three to six bedrooms, two or three bathrooms, accessible showers, and equipped kitchens. Many have pools fitted with lifts. ✆ 1-863-424-0795 • www.villasinorlando.com

6 Walker Medical & Mobility Products

The local franchise for Walker Medical & Mobility Products rents wheelchairs and three-wheel rechargeable electric scooters, including ones for people weighing more than 375 lbs (170 kg). They all fit into Disney's transport vehicles and can be taken apart to fit into cars. The company delivers to local hotels and houses. ✆ 407-331-9500 • www.walkermobility.com

7 Disney for Disabled Guests

The free Guidebook for Guests with Disabilities details special needs services, including: accessibility in parks; Braille directory locations; special-needs parking; wheelchair and electric-cart rentals; audio tours; and translator units for the deaf. They are available at Guest Services in all the theme parks or at Disney hotels' front desks. ✆ 407-824-4321 • www.disneyworld.com

8 Universal for Disabled Guests

Universal's parks and hotels have the following services: audio guides; wheelchair and scooter rentals; and telecommunications devices for the deaf. A free booklet is available from Guest Relations at park entrances and resort front desks. ✆ 407-363-8000 • www. universalorlando.com

9 SeaWorld for Disabled Guests

SeaWorld provides a Braille guide, plus a written synopsis of its shows and telecommunications devices for the hearing impaired. Most of its rides and shows are accessible. It rents wheelchairs and scooters. A small guidebook is available at Guest Relations. ✆ 407-351-3600 • www.seaworld.com

10 Society for Accessible Travel & Hospitality

Members pay an annual subscription for access to a range of services, but non-members can get information on travel for the disabled (including specific hotels and attractions) for a small fee. ✆ 1-212-447-7284 • www.sath.org

Left **Getting wet** Center **Kids' menu** Right **SeaWorld stroller rental**

TOP 10 Tips for Families

1 Name Tags & Reunion Places

It's very easy to get lost in crowded theme parks. If that happens, find a park employee (they're usually in uniform) and ask for help. Kids seven and under should wear tags bearing their name, hotel, and a contact number. Older kids and adults should pick a place inside the park to meet if they become separated.

2 Parent-Swaps

Height restrictions (see below) mean that some younger children may not be able to go on certain rides. The theme parks usually have a program that lets one parent ride while the other tends to the kids in a special waiting area. Then the second parent can go on the ride: it might not be so much fun riding by yourself but at least you don't have to wait in line again.

3 Stroller Rental & Baby Care

All the major theme parks offer stroller rental. There are also excellent nursing facilities, often with free formula provided. Diaper changing tables can be found in women's and some men's restrooms, and diapers are available free of charge at Universal's parks.

4 Breaks

Theme parks are tiring at any time of year, but excessively so in summer, when even standing in line can be exhausting. Plan regular breaks at air-conditioned venues (best visited around midday, when it's hottest outside), or "splash areas" (see below).

5 Refreshments

Bring snacks for energy and don't forget water. The parks have a few drinking fountains, but bottled water is very expensive.

6 Getting Wet & Not Getting Wet

Take a change of clothes to the theme parks, if not for yourself then for the children. Apart from water rides where you might expect to get wet, kids enjoy running through "splash areas" to cool off, and drying off naturally might not be possible. A rain poncho is smart year round, since Florida has rainy spells in both summer and winter.

7 Theme Park Ride Restrictions

Disney parks tend to have few health and height restrictions, although Disney-MGM Studios is a little restrictive. Universal's parks can be more limiting for younger kids, especially Islands of Adventure (with warnings on nine of the 13 major rides), but like Universal Studios, it has a dedicated kids' area. SeaWorld has height restrictions on a couple of rides, while at Discovery Cove, you must be at least six years old to swim with the dolphins. Non-swimmers can still join in, but obviously can't enjoy the full experience.

8 Children's Menus

Most of the more expensive and dressy restaurants discourage young diners either by failing to provide children's menus or with outright bans on anyone under 17 years of age. However, most restaurants have some kind of kids' menu, usually in the $4 to $6 range. Some also provide distractions such as crayons and coloring-in placemats.

9 Character Meals

Disney lures families with children to a dozen of their restaurants to charge exorbitant prices for eating breakfast, lunch, or dinner with humans dressed in Disney character costumes. Universal also has one "character" restaurant, and there are some similar set-ups outside of theme parks. See p71.

10 Kids Stay Free

Orlando is Kidsville. The little ones don't pay, but they're the reason adults do. Smart hoteliers let kids stay free. Most rooms have beds for four, so even if there are only two in the party, the extra beds are part of the deal.

Left **Rush hour on I-4** Right **Merritt Island National Wildlife Refuge**

Things to Avoid

1 Park Visits When School's Out

All the parks are packed during school breaks (late Jun–late Aug; late Dec–early Jan; mid-Feb, and Easter), since that's when locals hit the parks with their kids. Summer is the worst, since not only is it crowded, but it's also brutally hot. The least crowded months are November plus early and late February.

2 Theme Park Isolation

Don't spend every waking minute in Orlando's theme parks, because burn-out is inevitable. Make sure you take time to see Central Florida's natural attractions (see p82–5), smaller attractions (see p44–5), and museums (see p60–61).

3 Early Arrivals

It might seem smart to hit the theme parks as soon as they open, but it is not always the best plan. Kids who arrive early tend to collapse by 2pm and are a mess the rest of the day. Instead, take it easy in the morning and head for the parks in the afternoons and evenings. Temperatures are cooler and the parks take on a magical glow under the lights.

4 Inflexibility

Relax. It's a vacation. There are no prizes for those who joylessly cram

every single ride at their chosen theme park into one day. Make plans, but be flexible. Don't attempt to do everything on your list, and maybe save a few things for the next visit.

5 Big Meals In-Park

In general, theme-park food is bland and overpriced, so don't waste your main meal of the day on it. Instead, at Universal, check out the eateries on Citywalk (see p105); while at Disney, visit one of the excellent resort dining options, where you'll find that high-end restaurants offer great value. Parks allow same-day re-entry on single tickets – just be sure to get your hand stamped before leaving.

6 Free and Discount Tickets

There are a lot of offers floating around Orlando that sound too good to be true. If someone promises free or heavily discounted tickets, ask "What's the catch?", especially if they're promising a Disney ticket. Most are timeshare salespeople trying to get you to "buy" a week's holiday for the next 20 years. In some cases they have legitimate tickets, but most of the time you have to endure hours of sales pitches. Usually, such properties are overpriced.

7 Wearing Skimpy Bathing Suits at Water Parks

Ladies should consider one-piece suits at water parks since most of the best rides can quickly rip off a bikini top. Alternatively, wear a T-shirt over the bikini for added protection. Guys, for reasons not necessary to elaborate upon here, should avoid Speedos altogether.

8 Public Transport

Lynx buses might appear to be everywhere, but don't set your schedule by them, especially for longer trips. They stop frequently, are notoriously slow, and are generally ignored by locals.

9 Downtown's Westside

The area of Downtown south of Colonial Drive and west of I-4 is not a particularly safe place to wander around. Avoid it. But if you are going to a destination here, including the Greyhound Bus station, call a cab.

10 Rush Hour on I-4

Sometimes called "Orlando's Parking Lot", I-4 can get very congested, particularly during evening rush hour (3–6:30pm), as attraction employees head home. Disney-generated traffic on I-4, between Lake Buena Vista and US Hwy 192, has a life of its own. Traffic jams there can occur around the clock.

Left **Family-friendly motel** Right **View from hotel room**

TOP 10 Accommodation Tips

1 Bed & Sales Taxes
Hotels have an assortment of hidden add-ons that can come as a surprise when you get the bill. Charges for the mini-bar and pay-per-view movies are always inflated. But the sales tax *(see p132)* and bed tax can really add to the bill. Orange County, including the theme parks, I–Drive, and downtown Orlando, adds five per cent bed tax; Osceola County, which includes Kissimmee, adds 6 per cent; and Seminole County, which includes Sanford *(see p85)*, adds a 3 per cent tax. Don't forget to factor in these extras when determining your vacation budget.

2 Rack Rates
These are the rates no one should agree to pay for a room! They're the walk-in-and-ask rates anyone can get without a coupon or package, and without asking for a discount or special deal. They're used in this book to provide a guide price, but don't settle for them. Insist on a better deal – it is almost always possible.

3 Rooms with a View
Many properties charge more for a room that has a view of anything other than the parking lot or the building next door. Before you pay, consider how much time you will want to spend in your room.

4 The Pros of Staying with Mickey
The main benefits are proximity to the parks, access to the free Disney transportation system *(see p127)*, preferred tee times at Disney golf courses *(see pp54–5)*, and an easy way to break up the day by returning to base for a midday nap or swim.

5 The Cons of Staying with Mickey
Rates at Disney World Resorts are about 30 per cent more than comparable accommodation on the outside, the transportation system is slow, and if you don't have a car and don't take cabs, you tend to be stuck with Disney, including at meal times.

6 Types of Accommodation
Orlando has almost 107,000 hotel rooms. Most tend to be functional budget options, but there are plenty of upscale choices, too, from lavish resorts to one-off B&Bs and boutique hotels.

7 Booking Services
In addition to making independent reservations or dealing directly with Disney or Universal resorts, vacationers can use reservations networks to book rooms. Central Reservation Service (CRS), Orlando.com, and Vacation Works are three of the more popular ones. Ⓢ *Walt Disney World • 407-828-8101 • www.disney world.com* Ⓢ *Universal • 407-224-7000 • www.universalorlando.com* Ⓢ *CRS • 407-740-6442 • www.crshotels.com* Ⓢ *Orlando.com • 407-999-9800 • www.orlando.com* Ⓢ *Vacation Works • 407-396-1883 • www.vacation works.com*

8 Land-Sea Options
A different approach is to take a seven-day land-sea package that includes a stay at any one or more Disney resorts plus a Caribbean cruise. Ⓢ *Disney Cruise Line • 407-566-6921 • www.disneycruise.com*

9 Family-Friendly Motels
Most Orlando properties go the extra mile to make sure kids are treated like royalty. In fact, most let kids under 17 stay free with accompanying adults. Holiday Inn Family Suites *(see p145)* and Holiday Inn Sunspree *(see p145)* offer more than the usual child-friendly amenities.

10 In-Room Calls
Don't use the in-room phone to make any calls without knowing the billing policy. Some hotels offer free local calls, while others charge double or more the 35¢ cost of using an outside pay phone. Some impose a $1-plus service charge whenever the phone is used (including for toll-free numbers), in addition to long-distance rates.

➣ *For accommodation listings See pp142–9*

Left **Portofino Bay Hotel** Right **Hard Rock Hotel**

Disney & Universal Resorts

1 Disney's Grand Floridian Resort & Spa

Disney's top hotel is an opulent, early 20th-century New England-style resort. Expect a ragtime mood and intimate rooms that promise romance and great views. The resort also has a full spa, health club, and tennis courts. ◎ *4401 Floridian Way • Map F1 • 407-824-3000 • www. disneyworld.com • $$$$*

2 Disney's Board-Walk Inn & Villas

This re-created 1940s seaside village is Disney's smallest deluxe hotel. The rooms are delightfully quaint; if you want more space, villas are available too. It is ideally located for all the facilities and buzz of the BoardWalk. ◎ *2101 N. Epcot Resorts Blvd • Map G2 • 407-939-5100; www.disneyworld. com • $$$$*

3 Portofino Bay Hotel

This Universal resort is a replica of Italy's Portofino village, right down to the boats and "fishermen" in the harbor. The rooms are spacious and feature luxe bed linen. The *gelati* (ice cream) machines by the pool are another nice touch. Guests get to skip the line for rides and shows at Universal's parks. ◎ *5601 Universal Blvd • Map T1 • 407-503-1000 • www.universal orlando.com • $$$$*

4 Walt Disney World Dolphin

This Sheraton resort is on Disney property so offers some Disney perks, such as use of the free transportation system *(see p127)*. The 27-floor pyramid contains outsize sculptures, a waterfall, plus more than 1,500 suites and rooms. ◎ *1500 Epcot Resorts Blvd • Map G2 • 407-934-4000 • www. swandolphin.com • $$$$*

5 Walt Disney World Swan

With two 46-ft (14-m) swans gracing its roof, this hotel is hard to miss. The beach-themed rooms are a little smaller than at its sister hotel, the Dolphin, but Swan guests share some of the facilities and perks of the Dolphin, including a spa. ◎ *1200 Epcot Resorts Blvd • Map G2 • 407-934-3000 • www.swandolphin.com • $$$$*

6 Disney's Yacht Club Resort

The theme here is New England yacht club. Some of the 630 nautical-style rooms have views over a lake. Guests can walk to Epcot in about 10 minutes. ◎ *1700 Epcot Resorts Blvd • Map G2 • 407-934-7000 • www. disneyworld.com • $$$$*

7 Disney's Wilder-ness Lodge

Live oaks and yellow pines surround this lovely wooded resort, modeled on the Yosemite Lodge at Yosemite National Park. Some rooms overlook woodlands; the villas are roomy and come with kitchens. ◎ *901 W. Timberline Dr • Map F1 • 407-824-3200 • www.disney world.com • $$$– $$$$*

8 Disney's Port Orleans Resort

You can opt to stay in the French Quarter's colonial houses with iron balconies or in the Riverside's southern-style mansions. Gardeners love the landscaping, and shoppers like the location. ◎ *2201 Orleans Dr • Map F2 • 407-934-5000 • www. disneyworld.com • $$–$$$*

9 Hard Rock Hotel

Universal's second resort boasts Mission-style architecture and a rock 'n' roll theme. Rooms are attractive and comfortable; the best views are from those facing the lake. Guests get to skip the lines for rides and shows at Universal's parks. ◎ *5000 Universal Blvd • Map T1 • 407-363-8000 • www.universal orlando. com • $$$–$$$$*

10 Disney's Value Resorts

The All-Star Movies, All-Star Music, and All-Star Sports resorts have relatively small rooms, but rates here are the cheapest in Walt Disney World Resort. ◎ *407-934-7639 • Map G1 • www.disney world.com • $–$$*

Unless indicated, all hotels have DA, smoking rooms, A/C, pool, free parking and kids' accommodation, and accept credit cards

Price Categories

For a standard, double room per night (with breakfast if included), taxes and extra charges.

$	under $90
$$	$90–180
$$$	$180–260
$$$$	over $250

Villas of Grand Cypress

🔟 Luxury Hotels

1 Hyatt Regency Grand Cypress

This vast resort is one of Orlando's most amazing places to stay. The 18-story atrium has inner and outer glass elevators with great views, some rooms have whirlpool baths, and the resort boasts a golf course, horseback riding, tennis courts *(see p56)*, a beach, and plenty of nature, including a lake and waterfalls. ✪ *1 Grand Cypress Blvd • Map F2 • 407-239-1234 • www.hyatt grandcypress.com • $$$$*

2 Wyndham Palace Resort

The classy rooms at this, the largest Lake Buena Vista hotel, have either balconies with lake views or patios. Evergreen rooms are hypo-allergenic, and have air and water filter systems. The Top of the Palace bar offers free champagne to guests who go to enjoy the sunset. ✪ *1900 Buena Vista Dr • Map G2 • 407-827-2727 • www.wyndham. com • $$$–$$$$*

3 Villas of Grand Cypress

The Hyatt's sister property offers condos and town houses, plus some suites. Some accommodations have Roman tubs and patios. Amenities include a golf course, tennis courts, and an equestrian center *(see p56)*. ✪ *1 N. Jacaranda • Map F2 • 407-239-4700 • www.grand cypress.com • $$$–$$$$*

4 Cypress Glen

Owner Sandy Sarillo offers just two rooms – one a more typical B&B nest, the other a massive space that has a huge bathroom with glass-block walls and a whirlpool for two. Breakfast is included, rooms are smoke-free, and kids under 16 aren't permitted. ✪ *10336 Vista Oaks Court • Map F2 • 407-909-0338 • www.cyp glen.com • $$$$*

5 Renaissance Orlando Resort

Both the amenity-filled rooms and their marble bathrooms in this snazzy hotel are massive. Even the atrium, filled with aquariums, waterfalls, and palm trees, is 10 stories high. ✪ *6677 Sea Harbor Dr • Map T5 • 407-351-5555 • www.renaissancehotels. com • $$–$$$$*

6 Peabody Orlando

This hotel boasts an elegant feel, friendly staff, and a great location for I-Drive attractions. Home of the Peabody Ducks *(see p46)*, it has four rooftop tennis courts, as well as a health center. ✪ *9801 International Dr • Map T4 • 407-352-4000 • www.peabody-orlando. com • $$$$*

7 Marriott's Orlando World Center

The 2,000 rooms at this 28-story tower tend to be a bit smaller than others in this price category, but they come with plenty of in-room features. The resort boasts a wide array of facilities including a spa and the biggest pool in town. ✪ *8701 World Center Dr • Map G2 • 407-239-4200 • www.marriott-hotels.com • $$–$$$$*

8 Westin Grand Bohemian

Soft-as-clouds beds are one of this elegant downtown hotel's greatest selling points. Rooms are modern, and public areas display rare artworks. ✪ *325 S. Orange Ave • Map P3 • 407-313-9000 • www.grandbohe mianhotel.com • $$–$$$*

9 Summerfield Suites Lake Buena Vista

The friendly staff and size of the suites make this an attractive choice for those who want to be near to, but not in, the clutches of Mickey. Rates include continental breakfast, and all suites have kitchens. ✪ *8751 Suitside Dr • Map F2 • 407-238-0777 • www.summerfield-orlando.com • $$–$$$*

10 Disney's Animal Kingdom Lodge

Disney's newest resort resembles a South African game lodge in a semi-circular *kraal* (compound). Rooms have an African theme and some have views of a wildlife-filled savanna. ✪ *2901 Osceola Pkwy • Map G1 • 407-938-3000 • www.disneyworld. com • $$$–$$$$*

Left **Doubletree Guest Suites** Right **Four Points by Sheraton Orlando Downtown**

Mid-Price Hotels (A–G)

1 Best Western Lake Buena Vista Hotel

All rooms have balconies at this official Disney hotel, some of which overlook beautiful gardens bordering the lake. There's free transportation to Disney's major parks, and it's within walking distance of Marketplace, Pleasure Island, and West Side. ✪ 2000 Hotel Plaza Blvd • Map F2 • 407-828-2424 • www.downtowndisney hotels.com • $$–$$$

2 Caribbean Beach Resort

Disney's largest hotel (with 2,112 rooms) is split into five "villages": Aruba, Trinidad, Martinique, Barbados, and Jamaica, each with its own pool and sandy beach. The rooms are on the small side but are good value. ✪ 900 Cayman Way • Map G2 • 407-934-3400 • www.dis neyworld.com • $$–$$$

3 Celebration Hotel

The elegant lakefront rooms at this three-story, timber-framed resort offer a tranquil water-and-woodlands view. Facilities include an outdoor pool with Jacuzzi, a fitness center, and nature trails. There's an 18-hole golf course (see p54) too. ✪ 700 Bloom St • Map G2 • 407-566-6000 • www.cele brationhotel.com • $$–$$$$

4 Courtyard at Lake Lucerne

Downtown's best B&B has four period buildings, from the Victorian Norment-Parry Inn to the Art Deco Wellborn House, which has apartments and a honeymoon suite. ✪ 211 N. Lucerne Circle E • Map P3 • 407-648-5188 • www. orlandohistoricinn.com • No pool • $$–$$$

5 Courtyard by Marriott

A facelift in 1997 has made this a good choice on the Hotel Plaza strip. All the well-appointed rooms have Nintendos, and the glass elevator that scales the 14-story, plant-filled atrium makes for a more exciting ride than most. There's a free Disney shuttle. ✪ 1805 Hotel Plaza Blvd • Map F2 • 407-828-8888 • www.courtyard orlando.com • $–$$$

6 Darst Victorian Manor

This newly built, Victorian-style hotel overlooks Lake Helen. The Queen Victoria suite, with its crimson furnishings and four-poster bed, is the most inviting of the six rooms. Gourmet breakfasts can include spinach strata and potato pancakes. ✪ 495 Old Hwy 441 • Off map • 1-352-383-4050 • $$–$$$

7 Doubletree-Castle Resort

The towering spires of this themed hotel make it look like a fairytale castle – if castles came in pink and blue, that is. Its 216 rooms and seven suites come with big-screen TVs and Sony Playstations. The resort has a roof terrace, a fitness center, and two restaurants. ✪ 8629 International Dr • Map T2 • 407-345-1511 • www.doubletree hotels.com • $$–$$$

8 Doubletree Guest Suites

After being welcomed with home-made cookies, head to your cozy one- or two-bedroomed suite at this official Disney hotel. With a landscaped pool and a spa, you can't fail to relax. ✪ 2305 Hotel Plaza Blvd • Map F2 • 407-934-1000 • www.doubletree guestsuites.com • $$–$$$

9 Eó Inn

The best boutique hotel in town offers minimalist elegance with a personal touch. All rooms come with office facilities, and some overlook Lake Eola. Try the on-site spa (see p59) if in need of pampering. ✪ 227 N. Eola Dr • Map N3 • 407-481-8485 • www.eoinn.com • No pool • No smoking rooms • $$–$$$

10 Four Points by Sheraton Orlando Downtown

With its functional rooms, two pools, fitness facilities, and three restaurants, this hotel is a good base for those interested in Downtown's museum, club, and performing arts scene. ✪ 151 E. Washington St • Map P2 • 407-841-3220 • www.starwood. com • $$–$$$

Unless indicated, all hotels have DA, smoking rooms, A/C, pool, free parking and kids' accommodation, and accept credit cards.

Holiday Inn Family Suites Resort

Price Categories

For a standard, double room per night (with breakfast if included), taxes and extra charges.

$	under $90
$$	$90–180
$$$	$180–260
$$$$	over $250

10 Mid-Price Hotels (H–Z)

1 Holiday Inn Family Suites Resort

Children rule in this resort, which has Kidsuites (sleeping up to seven) with big-screen TVs. Other types of suite include Cinemasuites, with even bigger TVs, and there are spacious rooms as well. Activities offered range from karaoke to ping-pong. ⊗ *1450 Continental Gateway • Map G3 • 407-387-5437 • www.hifamily suites.com • $$*

2 Holiday Inn Sunspree Resort

If keeping the kids happy is top priority, this hotel is a good bet. Apart from the themed, two-roomed Kidsuites (space ship, tree house, igloo, and so on), there's a free activities program for 3–12 year olds. Children even have their own restaurant. ⊗ *13351 Apopka-Vineland Rd • Map G3 • 407-239-4330 • www. kidsuites.com • $$*

3 Homewood Suites Orlando

These modern luxury suites in neutral tones, with spacious living rooms and kitchens, can sleep up to six people. Free hors d'oeuvres, beer, and wine are served early evening in the lobby (Mon–Thu), and the rates include breakfast. ⊗ *8200 Palm Pkwy • Map F2 • 407-465-8200 • www.homewood-suites.com • No DA • $$*

4 Hotel Royal Plaza

The Plaza has had a partial makeover recently. Some of the rooms have whirlpools; pool-side ones have balconies or patios. The pool is heated and there's a spa, fitness center, and four lit tennis courts. ⊗ *1905 Hotel Plaza Blvd • Map F2 • 407-828-2828 • www.downtown disneyhotels.com • $$–$$$*

5 Radisson Hotel Universal Orlando

A $16 million renovation helped convert this former convention hotel into one that woos travelers who want to be near the Universal parks. The hotel's two towers house 742 modern rooms and suites; those on the west side overlook the parks and CityWalk. ⊗ *5780 Major Blvd • Map T2 • 407-351-1000 • www.radisson universal.com • $$–$$$*

6 Renaissance World Gate

Don't expect the normal Renaissance high standard, since the 577 rooms at this hotel are more motel-like. Still, price, location, and service make it attractive. ⊗ *3011 Maingate Lane • Map G2 • 407-396-1400 • www.renais sancehotels.com • $$*

7 Sierra Suites Hotel

Some of the 137 suites have wheelchair access, others are tailored to the hearing impaired. There's a heated pool, barbecues, and a Jacuzzi, and it's on the I-Ride Trolley circuit and provides a free shuttle to Disney. ⊗ *8750 Universal Blvd • Map E3 • 407-903-1500 • www. sierra-orlando.com • $$*

8 Springhill Suites Lake Buena Vista

This pleasant suite hotel located in the Marriott Village is close to Disney. All the suites have a king-size or two double beds, plus separate living and cooking areas. ⊗ *8623 Vineland Ave • Map G2 • 407-938-9001 • www. springhillsuites.com • $$*

9 Thurston House

Built in 1885, and set in woodland, this charming B&B offers a quiet retreat, popular with adults. The four rooms, with queen-size beds, overlook Lake Eulalia. It's smoke-free and has no pool, but the home-away-from-home atmosphere is a winner. ⊗ *851 Lake Ave • Map F3 • 407-539-1911 • www.thurston house.com • No DA • $$*

10 Veranda B&B

All five buildings in this charming downtown inn date from the early 1900s. Some rooms have balconies overlooking the garden courtyard, as well as four-poster beds. All rooms are smoke-free, and rates include daily continental breakfast. ⊗ *115 N. Summerlin Ave • Map Q3 • 407-849-0321 • www.theveranda-bandb. com • $$–$$$*

Left **Econo Lodge Maingate** Right **Quality Inn sign**

🔟 Inexpensive Hotels (A–G)

1 Best Western Eastgate

The rather basic rooms – as in most cheap chains – are small, but this five-story motel has a video games room, a playground, two tennis courts, and is not far from Disney. ⚓ *5565 W. Irlo Bronson Memorial Hwy • Map G2 • 407-396-0707 • www. bestwestern.com • $–$$*

2 Best Western Kissimmee

This three-story motel has moderate-sized rooms and is a good base if you're into sport and nature, with facilities and activities close by. In the restaurant, children under 10 eat free if accompanied by paying adults. ⚓ *2261 E. Irlo Bronson Memorial Hwy • Map H5 • 407-846-2221 • www. bestwestern.com • $*

3 Best Western Mount Vernon Inn

Located some 20 miles (32 km) north of Disney World, this is a cozy, colonial-style motel, with friendly staff. Some of the rooms have small sitting areas. There's a city park across the street and many of Downtown's cultural attractions are nearby. ⚓ *110 S. Orlando Ave • Map H4 • 407-647-1166 • www.bestwestern. com • $*

4 Comfort Inn Maingate West

The motel-style rooms (with two double beds) are on the small side, but the location, just west of Disney, is a plus. Breakfast included. ⚓ *9330 W. Irlo Bronson Memorial Hwy • Map G3 • 1-863-424-8420 • www.choicehotels.com • No smoking rooms • $*

5 Days Inn Convention Center North of SeaWorld

This branch of the Days Inn chain makes a good base for convention-goers and vacationers alike. The hotel is surrounded by landscaped grounds and has a pancake restaurant and playground. ⚓ *9990 International Dr • Map T5 • 407-352-8700 • www.days inn.com • $–$$*

6 Days Inn Orlando Lakeside

Cheap rates and a good location at the northern end of I-Drive are the selling points for this Days Inn. The rooms are small and basic; some have a lake view. ⚓ *7335 Sand Lake Rd • Map S3 • 407-351-1900 • www. daysinn.com • $*

7 Delta Orlando Resort

The Delta, at the entrance to Universal Studios, is situated in extensive grounds, home to tropical birds, a koi pond, and all manner of flora; the rooms are less inspiring but comfortable. Kids six years and under eat for free in the restaurant. ⚓ *5715 Major Blvd • Map U1 • 407-351-3340 • www. deltaorlandoresort.com • $*

8 Econo Lodge Maingate

The rooms at this Hawaiian-themed hotel (suited to families on a budget) are small, but some sleep five. The location – on Disney's doorstep – and affordability are a winning mix, but there's no elevator to get to upper-story rooms. ⚓ *7514 W. Irlo Bronson Hwy • Map G1 • 407-396-2000 • www.enjoyflorida hotels.com • $*

9 Fairfield Inn Orlando International Drive

The rooms are a step above most in this price category, and the majority are situated away from the noise of I-Drive traffic. The motel is located between Sea-World and the Universal parks, and it's on the I-Ride Trolley circuit *(see p127)*. Rates include continental breakfast. ⚓ *8342 Jamaican Ct • Map T3 • 407-363-1944 • www.fairfieldinn.com • $*

10 Fairfield Inn Winter Park

Marriott's budget option is a modern motel situated well away from the main tourist resorts. But its location is great for anyone interested in shopping as well as more cultural diversions. Rates include continental breakfast. ⚓ *951 Wymore Rd • Map B4 • 407-539-1955 • www.fairfieldinn. com • $*

Unless indicated, all hotels have DA, smoking rooms, A/C, pool, free parking and kids' accommodation, and accept credit cards.

Price Categories

For a standard, double room per night (with breakfast if included), taxes and extra charges.

$	under $90
$$	$90–180
$$$	$180–250
$$$$	over $250

Left **Best Western Mount Vernon Inn**

🔟 Inexpensive Hotels (H–Z)

1 Hampton Inn Maingate West

The Hampton Maingate has a newer and nicer feel than most hotels in this price bracket. Rooms are smallish but sleep up to four. There's a free Disney shuttle, and rates include breakfast and free local phone calls. ◈ 3000 Maingate Lane • Map G2 • 407-396-6300 • www.hampton innmaingatewest.com • $

2 H-I Orlando/ Kissimmee Resort

Orlando's only hostel is on picturesque Lake Cecile. Most of the rooms are dorms with six beds, but some private rooms are available. There's a picnic area, kitchen lockers, a laundry, and free use of paddle boats. ◈ 4840 W. Irlo Bronson Memorial Hwy • Map G3 • 407-396-8282 • www.hiorlando.org • No smoking rooms • Kids 3 & under stay free • $

3 Holiday Inn Express

Just one mile (1.6 km) from the Wet 'n Wild and Universal parks, this motel offers free transport to Disney. Its rooms – with two double beds – are no-frills but pleasant. Rates include breakfast. ◈ 6323 International Dr • Map T2 • 407-351-4430 • www.sixcontinents hotels.com/hiexpress • $

4 Howard Johnson Inn Maingate East

Rooms at this inn are of the motel variety – sparse and small, but they do come with Nintendo consoles. Ask for a room at the rear to escape the noise of traffic. One child eats free with each paying adult in the restaurant. Efficiencies (small serviced apartments) are available. ◈ 6051 W. Irlo Bronson Memorial Hwy • Map G2 • 407-396-1748 • www.hojomge.com • $

5 International Drive Travelodge

The Travelodge is a good choice for value-conscious guests who want to be in the heart of I-Drive's attractions. It's more upscale than some in this category and has a great tropical pool bar. ◈ 5859 American Way • Map T2 • 407-345-8880 • www.travelodge.com • $

6 Quality Inn Lake Cecile

Situated on Lake Cecile, this motel is five miles (8 km) from Mickey's place. The rooms are a bit cramped, but they have Nintendos. The inn has a sandy lakeside beach, with jet skis and water-skiing on offer. ◈ 4944 W. Irlo Bronson Memorial Hwy • Map H3 • 407-396-4455 • www.qualityinn lakececile.com • $

7 Quality Inn Plaza

This is a good-value place given its location on I-Drive, just opposite Pointe Orlando. The standard rooms are really quite small, so if space is an issue, opt for a semi-suite. Three pools, two games rooms, and a 24-hour deli are among the on-site amenities. ◈ 9000 International Dr • Map T4 • 407-996-8585 • www.qualityinn-orlando.com • $

8 La Quinta Inn & Suites UCF

This choice, near the University of Central Florida, is for guests who want an east Orlando location. Rooms are comfortable, and rates include breakfast, local phone calls, and weekday newspapers. ◈ 11805 Research Pkwy • Off map • 407-737-6075 • www.laquinta.com • $$

9 Ramada Inn Resort Eastgate

The Ramada's rooms have balconies, two double beds, and Nintendos. Kids 12 and under eat free with a paying adult. Facilities include basketball and tennis courts. ◈ 5150 W. Irlo Bronson Memorial Hwy • Map G3 • 407-396-1111 • www.ramada.com • $–$$

10 The Unicorn Inn

British-run, this B&B, in a building dating from 1901 is quaint, homey, and just a short stroll from Lake Tohopekaliga. There are only six, smallish, ensuite rooms so reserve well in advance. Breakfast is included, and a guest kitchen is available. ◈ 8 S. Orlando Ave • Map H4 • 407-846-1200 • No pool • No smoking rooms • $

For ways to have fun on the cheap **See pp46–7**

Left **Sheraton's Vistana Resort** Right **Beach Tree Villas**

Condo & Timeshare Rentals

1 Disney Vacation Club

The same upscale Disney units that are sold as time-shares are also available for rental. Properties are located at the Old Key West Resort (white clap-board houses), Boardwalk Villas (see p142), and Wilderness Lodge (see p142). Ⓢ 407-566-3100 • Map F2, G2 & F1 • www. dvcresorts.com • $$$$

2 Sheraton's Vistana Resort

This resort offers modern one- and two-bedroom villas and town houses, packed with home com-forts, that can be rented by the week. The tennis facilities are excellent, with both clay and all-weather courts. Ⓢ 8800 Vistana Center Dr • Map G2 • 407-239-3100 • www. starwood.com/sheraton • $$$–$$$$

3 Summer Bay Resort

Accommodation at Sum-mer Bay ranges from one-bedroom condos to three-bedroom villas; all have washers and dryers. The property has a clubhouse and offers a Friday-night luau (traditional Hawaiian meal). Ⓢ 17805 W. Irlo Bronson Memorial Hwy • Map G1 • 1-352-242-1100 • www.summerbayresort. com • $$–$$$$

4 Endless Summer Vacation Homes

This organization leases two- to five-bedroom

houses in several locations around Central Florida. All have their own pools; some are near golf links. You need to pay a pre-mium for any stays of less than seven nights. Ⓢ 3501 W. Vine St, Suite 131, Kissimmee • 407-870-1552 • www.esvflorida. com • $–$$$

5 Marriott Vacation Club International

Marriott's timeshare pro-gram covers five Orlando locations. The apartments and villas can also be rented by the week. Some of the villas have screened patios or porches, and facilities include activity programs, fitness centers, golf-course privileges, tennis courts, clubhouses, and saunas. Ⓢ 407-238-1300 • www.vacationclub.com • $$$–$$$$

6 Holiday Villas

For generous living space (although bedrooms are on the small side), Holiday Villas offers two- and three-bedroom condos that can sleep up to eight. Each comes with a washer and dryer. Ⓢ 2928 Vineland Rd • Map G3 • 407-397-0700 • www. holidayvillas.com • $$–$$$

7 Blue Tree Resort

Blue Tree's elegant and spacious one- and two-bedroom villas are well-located for Disney attractions. The resort has four pools, two tennis courts, a volleyball

court, and a playground. Rates are available with or without housekeeping services. Ⓢ 12007 Cypress Run Rd • Map F3 • 407-238-6000 • www.bluetree resort.com • $$–$$$

8 Villas at Polo Park

Polo Park, with its two- and three-bedroom villas, is a real home-away-from-home. It lacks the crowds and tourist frenzy of the mainstream areas. Ⓢ 12727 Hwy 27 N. • Off map • 1-863-420-3838 • www.orlandocondos.net • Smoke free • $

9 Island One Resorts

There are four themed resorts to choose from, offering roomy one- to three-bedroom condos and villas. Facilities vary, but range from whirlpools to nature trails, and they sell discount attraction tickets. Ⓢ 2345 Sand Lake Rd, Suite 100 • 407-859-8900 • www.islandone. com • $$–$$$$

10 Beach Tree Villas

Great for families, the Beach Tree has two- to five-bedroom homes, the larger of which have private pools. There's an on-site recreation center, sauna, and a tennis court, but rates don't include an extra cleaning fee. Villas have a four-night mini-mum stay; houses have a five-night minimum. Ⓢ 2545 Chatham Circle • Map G3 • 407-396-7416 • www.beachtreevillas.com • Smoke free • $–$$$$

Price Categories

For a standard, double room per night (with breakfast if included), taxes and extra charges.

$	under $90
$$	$90–180
$$$	$180–250
$$$$	over $250

Left **Fort Summit Orlando KOA Kampground**

🔟 Close to Nature

1 Fort Wilderness Resort & Campground

Vast tracts of cypress and pine trees, fish-filled lakes, and fresh air envelop this Disney resort. It has 783 tent sites plus 409 cabins, which sleep up to six and have kitchens (the newer ones also have sun decks). Canoeing and horseback riding are two of the many outdoor activities on offer. ◎ 4510 N. Fort Wilderness Trail • Map F1 • 407-824-2900 • www.disneyworld.com • $$$–$$$$

2 Villas at Disney Institute

The options here include one-bedroom bungalows, two-bedroom town houses, fairway villas next to Disney golf courses, and three-bedroom Treehouse Villas that are 10 ft (3 m) off the ground. Most include daily housekeeping and there are lots of recreation choices. ◎ 1960 Magnolia Way • 407-827-1100 • www.disneyworld.com • $$$$

3 Southport Park Campground & Marina

This relaxing park is in 25-acres (10 ha) of lakeside woods. While away time on site by fishing, wandering among the wildlife (such as eagles and deer), or by taking an airboat trip. There are RV and tent sites with full hook-ups. ◎ 2001 W. Southport Rd • 407-933-5822 • www.southportpark.com • $

4 Floridian RV Resort

This woodsy retreat near Lake Tohopekaliga offers full hook-ups for RVs, two clubhouses, a playground, tennis courts, and a volleyball court. There are plenty of leisure activities in the area, such as airboat rides and parasailing ◎ 5150 Boggy Creek Rd • Off map • 407-892-5171 • www.florida-rv-parks.com • $

5 Orlando SW/Fort Summit KOA

A great place to camp if you want to be close to Walt Disney World and SeaWorld. There are RV sites, camp sites, and cabins. RV sites can have cable TV and modem dataport connected for an extra charge. ◎ PO Box 22182, Lake Buena Vista • 1-888-562-4712 • www.koa.com/where/fl/09327.htm • $

6 Clerbrook Golf & RV Resort

This large site, popular with golfers, offers 1,250 RV hook-ups, non-smoking villas, plus amenities including a driving range, four whirlpools, a library, and a beauty salon. ◎ 20005 Hwy 27 • Off map • 1-352-394-5513 • www.florida-rv-parks.com • $

7 Cypress Cove Nudist Resort

Unself-conscious couples and families, with either American Association for Nude Recreation or Cypress Cove resort membership, stay in villas, rooms, and RV sites here. ◎ 4425 Pleasant Hill Rd • Off map • 407-933-5870 • www.suncove.com • $–$$

8 Fort Summit Orlando KOA Kampground

This resort offers full hook-ups for RVs, as well as small timber cabins and pitches for tents. There's a store, laundromats, and internet access. ◎ 2525 Frontage Rd • Off map • 1-863-424-1880 • www.fortsummit.com • $

9 Circle F. Dude Ranch Camp

This kids' summer camp is also a family retreat on selected weekends between November and May. Hay rides, horseback riding, lake swimming, and sailing are some of the activities on offer. Weekend rates include five meals. ◎ Hwy 60 & Dude Ranch Rd • Off map • 1-863-676-4113 • www.circle-f-duderanch.com • smoke-free • No DA • $$ (per cabin for two nights)

10 Orlando Winter Garden RV Resort

Pines and ponds are all around this RV resort, about a 30-minute drive from Disney World. It boasts lots of facilities such as laundry, games room, dances, bingo, and barbecues. Popular with an older crowd. ◎ 13905 W. Colonial Dr • Map C1 • 407-656-1415 • www.florida-rv-parks.com • $

General Index

Acknowledgements

The Authors
Richard Grula lives in Orlando and specializes in writing about the downtown and cultural scenes. He's contributed to the *Orlando Weekly, Orlando Magazine, Sidewalk.com,* and *Time Out's Guide to Miami and Orlando.*

Jim and Cynthia Tunstall are Central Florida natives who have written five other Florida guides, including Frommer's *Walt Disney World & Orlando.*

Produced by Departure Lounge, London
Editorial Director Naomi Peck
Art Editor Lee Redmond
Editor Clare Tomlinson
Designer Lisa Kosky
DTP Designer Ingrid Vienings
Picture Researcher Monica Allende
Research Assistance Amaia Allende, Ana Virginia Aranha, Diveen Henry, Faiyaz Kara
Proofreader Stephanie Driver
Indexer Hilary Bird
Fact Checker Faiyaz Kara

Photographers Gregory Matthews, Magnus Rew

Illustrator Lee Redmond

Maps John Plumer

AT DORLING KINDERSLEY
Senior Publishing Manager
Louise Bostock Lang
Publishing Manager Kate Poole
Senior Art Editor Marisa Renzullo
Director of Publishing Gillian Allan
Publisher Douglas Amrine
Cartography Co-ordinator Casper Morris
DTP Jason Little, Conrad van Dyk
Production Sarah Dodd

Picture Credits
Placement Key: t-top; tc-top centre; tr-top right; cla-centre left above; ca-centre above; cra-centre right above; cl-centre left; cc-centre; cr-centre right; clb-centre left below; cb-centre below; crb-centre right below; bl-below left; bc-below centre; br-below right.

Every effort has been made to trace the copyright holders, and we apologize in advance for any unintentional omissions. We would be pleased to insert the appropriate acknowledgements in any subsequent edition of this publication.

This book makes reference to various Disney copyrighted characters, trademarks, marks and registered marks owned by The Walt Disney Company and Disney Enterprises, Inc.

The publishers would like to thank the following individuals, companies and picture libraries for permission to reproduce their photographs:

Index of Main Streets

Street Index